COPY THIS IDEA

He started a little part-time business
in his spare room at home...

It quickly made him a multimillionaire

" *I buy something for £5...*
and I sell it for over £50...

I buy something else for £50...
and I sell it for almost £2000...

And I can do it 100s of times
in a single month! "

Now you can copy this down-to-earth guy
who escaped the 9–5 rat race and
banked over 50 million pounds!
Starting in his spare room

COPY THIS IDEA

Kick start your way to making big money from your laptop at home, on the beach or anywhere you choose

Andrew Reynolds

CAPSTONE

Contents

Preface

It's Not Just About The **Money**

My Mum couldn't hide her tears and she turned and sobbed with joy, hugging me tightly, still clutching the 'new home' card I'd bought her, in which I'd written simply:

'Welcome Home. Love from Andrew. x'

'Thank you', she wept. 'I don't know how to thank you enough – I will never be able to repay you.' We just stood there in her new lounge, hugging and both crying.

How things had changed!

This was my Mum, who'd brought me into the world, living in a one-bedroom caravan, scraping by day-to-day, barely above the poverty line … the woman who had gone without so much in her life to make sure I was fed and clothed as a child – and now I'd just paid cash to buy her an elegantly furnished, half-a-million-quid town house to live in.

It was amazing to be able to do this for her, something I'd always promised I would do one day if I ever found a way to make a load of money. Had I not been able to, she'd have ended up in her later years with no money, struggling to get by day after day, as she had done her whole damn life.

Earlier that crisp February morning in 2007, I had pulled up in my Bentley outside her tiny old two-up two-down house and had picked her up to drive her here to a whole new life. She stepped out of the car, popped on her coat and looked up at the three-story, four-bedroom town house. She looked at me, then back up at the house, with a tear in her eye as if to say: 'is this really all mine?'

The furnishers and interior designers had been in. They'd done a great job over the previous few weeks. Everything smelt wonderfully fresh as we stepped inside – a welcome change from that damp and musty smell that had filled our old home where I grew up. Mum sighed, taking everything in as we both walked, having slipped off our shoes, from room to room – taking in the décor, the plush carpets, the furnishings, the fabrics and the prints. Everything was brand new. It was such an incredible change from being able to afford only second-hand furniture, and just 'making do'.

My mother had never had much. She had gone without for most of her adult life as she raised her family. She had no fridge, freezer or washing machine until I was about 14, having instead to boil washing in a bucket on the gas cooker. She had no central heating in her home until she was about 60 years old! She'd sacrificed a lot to feed and clothe us; to make sure that my brother and I were OK. We were certainly happy children and rarely felt affected by the relentless struggle of being broke that my parents endured throughout their adult lives. We went to school on the local council estate and, although none of the families on the estate could be considered well off, my brother and I were probably among the poorer ones, financially, in school. Our clothes consisted more or less of what we stood up in, plus a few items handed down from a cousin of mine, or items handmade by my Gran. That was the just the way it was.

In fact, as a 12 year old, I owned just one bright yellow roll-neck jumper to wear outside of school, which Mum had knitted for me. One day she'd washed it and had been drying it on top of a paraffin heater that we had in our kitchen to try to keep us all warm – and had accidentally burnt the collar. We didn't have enough money to buy a new jumper, so she unpicked the collar and re-knitted it into an open-necked sweater. She was resourceful like that … she had to be.

My parents spent their whole lives together struggling, just to get by, on Dad's meagre earnings. For seven years after getting their first house they had no furniture in the lounge and had to make do with a hand-me-down dining table and chairs and second-hand curtains.

Mum very rarely cried in front of us. Bursting into tears that day in her new home revealed her sheer relief and joy at never *ever* needing to go without again. The feeling of financial security that she'd longed for throughout her countless years of struggling had finally arrived. She was safe, secure and able to enjoy life at long last.

It was the first time since my father passed away seven years previously that she'd actually had the chance to live in a nice house with beautiful things all around her. Mum is passionate about painting and music, but her creative side was suppressed for most of her life. She was too busy working full time in the family hardware shop, bringing us up and taking care of the cooking and cleaning in the house. Of course, even if she'd managed to find the time in her busy day, she never had any money to spare to pay for paints or other art materials.

Now, though, she loves to paint. She has her own art room for painting … and her own music room for her piano. She has taken up learning the harp too. Her life *is* her art and her music. Indeed, it always would have been, had she been free to follow her dreams and express the real her. It always would have been – if only she'd had the money!

As Mum and I stood in her brand new lounge with our arms around each other for what seemed like hours, I thought about how my parents had struggled to make ends meet for their entire lives together. It was at that very moment that making my £ millions meant the most to me: it gave me the opportunity to do something life-changing for the kind and selfless woman who had brought me up against all odds. It enabled me to replace her life-long financial struggles with a luxurious, spacious new home and financial freedom. It enabled her to really 'live' the life she was born for.

All because I stumbled upon a little-known way to make money from my spare room at home …

The **First** Million

I absolutely knew this was what I had been looking for…

When I was asked to write this book, I remember my publisher saying to me – 'You're nothing special, yet you've made all this money!'

And she was right. I'm nothing special. I'm not some glitzy TV business guru or someone whose face you see every other day in the papers. I'm nothing special – I'm just an ordinary bloke who keeps himself to himself … who left school with four GCSEs – including woodwork and drawing. I'm not an expert on the world of business and you certainly won't find me at one of those awful business networking events.

No, I'm just an ordinary bloke who was bored with his full-time job, the commuting in traffic, the bosses I hated and the 'just getting by each month', and stumbled upon a great way for someone with no business qualifications and no experience, to start and run a business in his spare room at home … and banked well over £50 million!!

It's a far cry from where I came from and what I grew up with. I was born and raised in a one-bedroom caravan by my parents, who could best be described as 'potless' for most of their lives.

They spent their adulthood scraping a living together in a little hardware store they ran at the bottom of the town. I went to school on the local council estate and never did very well. My Dad wanted me to go into the family business – so I was packed off to the local technical college when I left school, to learn about business. But I was a failure. I remember the look of absolute bewilderment on the face of the lecturer who used to teach us accountancy. Seems I was the only person <u>ever</u> to fail the accountancy exam. What made it a real kick in the teeth, as far as he was concerned, was that HE wrote the exam paper – HE told us what to revise ... and yet I STILL failed!! He was beside himself. It wasn't my fault. I simply didn't understand what the rows of figures on a balance sheet meant. In fact, I still don't – even now!

> **I buy something for £5 and sell it for £50 ... I buy something for £50 and sell it for almost £2000**

I understand that if I **buy something for £5 and sell it for £50** – or I **buy something for £50 and sell it for almost £2000** (which I do all the time in my business) – there's a nice chunk of profit in there. (In this book I'll show you the money-making system I use – and how you can copy my way of making these huge profits for yourself if you wish.)

But when my accountant calls in to go through my annual accounts and starts banging on about accruals and cash movements, I just glaze over. (My last accountant, by the way, went out of business. A quick word of caution: never take advice on business from an accountant. Accountants keep the score – many of them actually don't know how to play the game!)

I honestly don't understand accounts and, despite what they teach you in business books, *you* don't have to understand them either. To be successful in business, you do not need

3

a deep understanding of how to manipulate numbers. You simply need to find someone who has a great way of making money … do all you can to learn what he or she does … and see if you are able to copy what they do for yourself.

Now I'm not talking about wholesale ripping off of somebody's products and selling pirate copies. That's simply illegal. However, in this book I'll share with you a system that I use (and that many of my successful students use too) to make a lot of money without working full time, without running a large corporate-style business, and without having to know the intricacies of accounts.

Back to the story – so we can get on …

Having never amounted to much at school, I drifted from one dead-end job to the next: working in a shop (following in Father's footsteps, I guess); as a trainee estate agent; selling caravans and mobile homes; and even dragging a huge suitcase of soft toys and dolls around, in my job as a rep for a toy manufacturer.

I eventually settled in the housebuilding industry and worked my way up, from a trainee to a decent job with a company car.

But, as I moved up the ladder, the more I grew to hate my job. I hated the daily commute (often two to three hours a day sat on motorways breathing in the fumes) … I hated a lot of the tasks I was given to do … and I didn't particularly like some of the people I worked for. Yet I stuck with it, completely trapped by the 'system'. You know, the thing we have all been brought up to believe in: you get a good job, you strive for promotion, you move up the ladder … and it's not just work. You move up the property ladder too – you take on a large mortgage so you have a nice house, you load up the credit card with debts for the things you think you need. Then, you wake up one day and find yourself on some sort of treadmill – working all month just to pay the bills – and then you go back and do the same thing again, month after month!

> **I always had a gut feeling that someone somewhere knew a better way to live – a better way to earn money.**

All the time I was working for someone else – **I always had a gut feeling that someone somewhere knew a better way to live – a better way to earn money** so that they had more freedom, more time to themselves, more time for what's important in life. I used to dream about not being rudely awoken by the alarm clock every morning, about not having to drive for hours and, most of all, about having enough money so I could pay off my debts and have my freedom.

For years I searched for that alternative. I answered some of those ads you see in the papers – the *get-rich-quick* schemes – promising the earth and then never delivering. I looked at all the existing businesses for sale in the papers too. But most of them were for sale because the owner wanted to unload his failing business onto someone else. In most cases I found that the businesses were actually making the owner less than I was earning as a salary – yet they wanted tens of thousands of pounds (hundreds of thousands in some cases) for me to purchase what amounted to a lower-paid job!

I looked at franchises – where you put down a load of money and buy into a business model that is proven. But – apart from the fact that I had little or no money to invest in a business – I really wasn't attracted to the types of business these franchise companies were offering: mobile dog washing, mobile wheelie bin cleaning, carpet cleaning or running a doughnut shop or burger joint. It just wasn't what I wanted out of life.

But I knew in my gut that the answer was out there somewhere. I just needed to find it.

Just at the point where I had really had enough – I was so desperately unhappy with my life – almost out of the blue I received an invitation to go to a three-day seminar, the topic of which was 'making money'. Now, this seminar wasn't just down the road – it was around 5000 miles away in Nevada, USA. Problem was, I received the invitation on a Saturday and the seminar was in just three days' time, on the following Tuesday. There was no way I could go … no way I could take a week off work at short notice and fly halfway across the world, particularly based on an email invitation to something that could turn out to be of little use.

That night I couldn't sleep. Again, some gut instinct told me that this was important; that this was something I had to do;

that the seminar would introduce me to something I needed to fulfil my dream.

So, on the Sunday morning, I called my boss at home (very much frowned upon – no one _ever_ did that!). I think I got him out of bed. I told him I had been invited to go to the States at short notice and, after a bit of discussion, my boss actually agreed that I could go. I couldn't believe it.

So, 48 hours later, I found myself, extremely jetlagged and shaken, sitting in a conference room on the other side of the world as the first speaker was introduced up onto the stage.

If I recall correctly, the subject of his talk was 'How to make $30,000 a month working from home'. I scribbled furiously in the hardback notebook that I'd bought that morning in the local drugstore – jotting down every single little idea I could, whilst the guy on stage talked. I drew little light bulbs by the side of things that particularly got my attention. I can tell you – that notebook, which I still have 15 years later, is crammed full of light-bulb doodles.

This guy on stage wasn't what I expected – he wasn't some glitzy, huge white smile and slick haircut, all-American 'Make Money Doin' Nothin' Guru' trying to sell us anything. There was no hype to him – he was a very ordinary, down-to-earth kind of guy, wearing old blue jeans and bright white trainers as he stood on stage, explaining how he'd started and how he ran a little business in his spare time working at home, making well over $30,000 a month from it.

I was hooked. My gut was in somersault mode that evening.

Most of the seminar delegates had gone off for dinner in the high-end restaurants around town, but I was having to watch the pennies, as I'd already loaded up the credit card for the flight and hotel, etc. So I sat with my notebook and pen, in the local food court eating the 'three items and a soda for $3.99' meal on a polystyrene plate with plastic cutlery, from the China Wok outlet.

As I went back over my notes from this guy's talk – I absolutely knew this was what I had been looking for.

I couldn't wait to get back on the plane – to head home and get started. A few days later, I walked nervously into my boss's office and said 'Can I have word?' I shut the door (something almost no one ever did, except *his* boss). I told him I was not happy and handed him my resignation. (By the way, that's a crazy and foolhardy thing to do and not something I would recommend you do today. The beauty of the system I'm sharing with you in this book is that you can set your new business up and just run it in your spare time. If you already have a job, keep that going until the money you make from your new business brings in more than the job – then hand in your notice. The beauty of the business I'll show you is that you can run it evenings and weekends – just in odd hours to suit you. You don't need to work full time on the business to get it up and running.)

Of course, I had to work my notice period at work, so that's what I did – I set up the business in my spare time, round the day job, so that it was ready when I eventually left work. And I also started to show other people what I was doing.

One of the first people I shared my excitement with was my Dad. I showed him what I had in mind. But I got no look of excitement back – no sparkle in his eyes … no 'wow!'

Instead he had a serious expression on his face, almost frowning, as he told me bluntly 'That won't work, son'.

You see, Dad's experience in life had been struggling to make enough money to feed the family – living hand to mouth each day, running his little hardware store.

His experience of business was based on what he had done – and what his father before him had done. My Dad ran a shop. And he never made a lot of money. I can still picture him now, at exactly 9 a.m., sweeping off the front step and the pavement outside his shop door, turning round the hanging 'OPEN' sign, then settling behind his counter with a cup of coffee, waiting for the first customer to wander in. Some days he'd wait in all morning before anyone turned up. Even then it might be for just a packet of screws or a bag of coal.

My Dad had been brought up on the idea that to be in business you need premises of some sort, with your name above the door. In his case, you rented yourself a shop (or bought it using a large loan). You then fill it full of stock, all bought on credit from the local wholesalers. You saddle yourself with a monthly rent to the landlord, business rates to pay, bills for lighting, heating, phones – you take on staff, you fit out your shop with shelving, cash registers, carrier bags with your name printed on the side, and all of the other 'stuff' needed just to open your shop to the public. And you spend or commit to most of that expenditure **BEFORE** you open on day one – before you even know if you have the right products for your customers and whether they will beat a path to your door.

It was a business that never made any money.

So when I showed my Dad what I had in mind – the business that I'd been shown by a guy in the US making more in a month than my Dad made in a whole year with his shop – he simply didn't believe it was possible. You may feel the same right now – thinking this might be 'too good to be true' – and I understand your scepticism. But, by the time you've read through the pages of this book, you will know without a doubt that there really is someone out there who found a better way to make money – and I'm going to lay it out for you, so that you can copy for yourself what I do.

Sharing what I do and allowing you to copy it, by the way, won't harm my own business one little bit. Far from it. In Chapter 8, you'll see how I've allowed several others to copy my business idea and some of them have gone on to bank over £1 million and become members of my Inner Circle – members of which I do joint ventures with. But we'll get to that later. First, back to the story …

Having had a knock-back from my Dad – telling me there was no way that this money-making idea of mine would work – I showed it to some of the guys at work as well. I remember one of them, an accountant, saying 'You've handed in your notice for this? Are you mad? This'll never work.'

I wonder what that old colleague is doing now. Again, his experience in life was that you work your way up the promotion ladder and get a better job, to pay for a better-looking house and a better-looking car (all on credit of course). He had no idea about running a real business for himself.

> I followed my gut – followed the system I had been shown, tweaked it and adapted it for the UK and starting from the spare room in my little three-bed semi on the local housing estate: so far I have banked over **£50 million**.

But, thank God, I followed my gut instinct. If I'd listened to the people giving me the benefit of their experience I would probably still be working for a living in the housebuilding industry – still paying a huge mortgage … still living month to month financially and dreading the credit card bills coming through the post.

I followed my gut – followed the system I had been shown, tweaked it and adapted it for the UK and starting from the spare room in my little three-bed semi on the local housing estate: so far I have banked **over £50 million**.

I remember when I first had a call from my accountant telling me that **I was now a cash millionaire** (in other words – not a millionaire on paper like some of those start-up experts talk about – where perhaps the theoretical value of the shares you own in the company you started, are now worth £1 million – and might be worth ten quid next week when something major goes wrong). I'm talking about having **£1 million cold, hard cash sat in your personal bank account!**

After my accountant called me with the news, I went to visit my Mum in her little two-up two-down house that she'd moved to after my Dad passed away. I hugged her and told her I had some news. I remember saying 'You're not going to believe this – but I am now a millionaire'. She stood back and stared at me – a look of suspicion on her face. I was right – she didn't believe me! 'What is it you're doing? I don't see how you can make £1 million in just a couple of years. Me and your father took a lifetime in the shop and we never made a penny. How can you make so much in such a short time?'

Turns out, she thought I was selling drugs!

It was only a few years later when I joined her for lunch in the VIP box at the O2 Arena in London, where she'd just watched me on stage at my **Entrepreneurs Bootcamp** event that I held to raise money for a children's charity, and she'd seen me talking to around 8000 attendees, explaining how my 'system' works – that she finally understood how her son makes money (and its certainly not selling drugs or doing anything illegal).

By the way, if you'd like to see some of that presentation filmed live at the O2 – I'd love to send you a free DVD of it, together with some other material that will help you once you've finished reading this book. As a thank you for reading this book, go to WWW.FREE-PACKAGE.COM and let me know where you'd like me to send it.

On stage at the O2 I'd mentioned how, when I was a kid, my Dad took me to London to see the sights. We went to Downing Street, where I stood on the step of Number 10 (you could do that back in my childhood days), and we went to see Buckingham Palace. I remember peering through the railings of the huge palace gates and my Dad telling me 'that's not for the likes of you or I son. That's for very important people, not us.'

I talked on stage about the thrill, 45 years later, of being driven through those same gates, in a chauffeur-driven Bentley, to attend a dinner at the palace to celebrate 30 years of the Prince's Trust, of which I was a patron. I explained how the car drove effortlessly around the central quadrangle within the palace grounds and how, as the car door was opened by a waiting member of the palace staff, I walked up the red carpet into the grand entranceway. I remember at the time looking up and saying quietly to myself, with a little tear forming in my eye … 'Well Dad, I made it!' and I reflected on how life had changed so much since those days of helping him in his little hardware shop, waiting around in the freezing cold for customers to come in to be served.

From the stage at that O2 presentation I wanted to demonstrate in a simple way how the business system I use is so fundamentally different from the one that most traditional businesses use – so I used the example of Dad's shop.

In his shop, Dad had maybe 16,000 items of stock – all bought on a large overdraft he had with the bank. Shelves full of every possible item of hardware you could think of, in all shapes and sizes. Huge display racks with every conceivable size of screw, nut and bolt, nail and hook – all bought on credit in the hope that someone would pop in to buy and that we would have the correct size of item that they wanted.

Contrast that with my business that I'm sharing with you in this book. When I started, I didn't have to have any stock at all. My customers would send me a payment (either a cheque in the post or online through PayPal or a similar card payment site). If, for example, they were buying a CD from me … once I had their order and payment, I would run off a copy of the CD on my PC, stick a label on it, place it in a CD case that I'd bought on eBay, pop it in a jiffy bag and take it to the local Post Office.

I could do that without having to pay for shop premises, without business rates, lighting bills, staff and all the other crippling overheads my Dad had in his business. I could run off the day's orders in the evening and pop them into the Post Office in my lunch hour. No waiting around all day in the hope that a customer might call in to buy something they wanted.

Of course, that was when I was just starting out, working on a shoestring and doing everything myself to save money.

Today, things are even easier. I don't have to handle any of the products; I don't have to deal with the orders; I don't have to speak to customers. I have all of that done on autopilot for me, by what's called a 'fulfilment house'. These companies do everything for you. They process the orders; they pop the products into jiffy bags or boxes; they deal with order despatching via Parcelforce, UKMail, Fedex or one of the other parcel companies; they process phone calls and queries; they handle any returns; and, at the end of the month, they send me a cheque minus their small % for their charges.

In this way I can run my business from my laptop or tablet, from almost anywhere in the world – and I can handle hundreds of orders a day, through having everything arranged via a fulfilment house.

Of course, I could still do all of the work myself – but by copying my business idea, you'll find that what is important is not just the money, but also the freedom and lifestyle that the business can bring.

I can still see my Dad spending 25 years of his life in that same shop, looking out of the same windows at the world passing by, waiting for customers to decide to spend a few pounds with him.

My big regret is that he passed away before I ever got to show him how successful this business is and how he could have copied what I do, for himself. It would have turned his life around completely.

It's a sad irony that the first thing I bought, when I'd paid off my mortgage and all of the credit card bills, was a luxurious BMW 7 Series car; and that the first time I got to drive it was to my Dad's funeral.

So, I missed the opportunity to show him that my business idea had worked so well and to share it with him so he could do the same. In this book I'd like to share it with you instead – to show you a different way to make money and to live a lifestyle where you are not trapped by the bills, where you won't spend your life looking out of the same window of a shop or an office.

My Dad loved to be near the sea. He always dreamed of having a house there. But he never got to achieve his dream. He spent most of his adult life in that cold, damp and dusty shop, dreaming of sitting by the sea listening to the waves – and the better life he'd have one day. He never got to see it.

This morning, I am writing this chapter from the balcony of my own house, which is set right on a private beach overlooking the sea. The sun is bursting through the clouds. The only sounds are the gently lapping waves, the seagulls, the soft throbbing sound of the engine of the little red lobster boat, chugging along in the distance collecting the day's catch, and my laptop keys as I write. Every day, the scene outside my windows is different – one day large, heavy storm clouds, the next the most spectacular sunrise or a full moon over the gently glistening sea. I can stroll into the local town for a light breakfast and relax, safe in the knowledge that over at the fulfilment house orders are coming in, customers are being looked after well and money is being deposited in my account.

It's a great way to live and, over the next few pages, I'd like to show you what I do so you can copy it for yourself if you'd like to.

Now don't expect some business book full of complicated five-year forecasts and sample business plans. In 15 years I've never compiled a business plan – never written a forecast. Leave all that stuff to the students who study business at university, and then get a shock when they enter the real world.

In this book I'd like to show you a different way to make money and to live a lifestyle where you are not trapped by the bills, where you won't spend your life looking out of the same window of a shop or an office.

Back in my housebuilding days we had to produce forecasts. We had so many charts and spreadsheets, on countless bits of paper, forecasting to the finest detail what would happen over the next five years, that no one was focused on making money right now, today. Oddly enough, the company I had been working for got taken over six months after I handed in my notice, because it was doing so badly. When I left that job I swore I would never do a forecast again. And I've stuck to that.

So, this book is not about business plans or forecast models. And neither is it a book containing loads of quotations and clever business buzzwords and phrases.

I'm just an ordinary, down-to-earth bloke who stumbled upon a great way to make money – and I've laid out what I do in this book so you can copy any or all of the ideas I've presented here.

Why would I do that?

Simple. In the past, I have shared my business ideas with a few others through workshops I have held. Some of the students from those workshops have then taken those ideas and successfully started their own businesses using what I shared with them. They all made money.

And, as their businesses grew, they then came back to me and asked if I would consider joint venturing projects with them – either them selling some of my products, or me selling some of theirs – for a 50/50 share of the profits.

I often have projects that I'm offered, that I don't have time to do myself. Again, it's all about the lifestyle – not about crazily cramming in as many projects as possible to make even more millions. There has to be a balance. Often I have projects that I turn away because I only want to do so many per year. So, I'm happy to joint venture such projects with serious students of mine who have proved themselves by getting their new business up and running, copying what I do. I get a share of the profits on a project I don't have time to do – they get profits they would otherwise not have had too. To use that overdone business cliché – it's a true *win–win*.

Now I'm not promising anything. I'm not promising that you will become a millionaire through copying what I do. (How could I? I don't know you personally – though I hope to talk to you one day when you have made a success of your new business.) I have no way of knowing what you will do with what I am sharing in this book.

But I know the **system works**.

It's worked for several of my students: like the **ex-call centre worker** who is now a full-time mum at home. She **banked over £1 million from her kitchen table**. Or the **musician** who attended one of my workshops and learned my system. He's **banked over £7 million** so far and shows no sign of stopping. Or the **DJ who banked over £3 million** just using what I taught him, and moved from his rented terraced house in the wrong part of town to a lovely five-bedroom detached house with a big sweep-in, sweep-out driveway and a large triple garage that he has converted into a nice home office from which he now runs his business.

These were all just ordinary individuals like you or me – with no experience, without huge amounts of money to start a business – who took my system, copied it and each went on to bank at least £1 million.

So, the system works. But, as I mentioned, I have no way of knowing what you will do with it. So this is not a guaranteed *get-rich-quick* book.

This is an ordinary bloke laying out, in what I hope is an easy-to-read fashion, the simple business idea that I have used to bank over £50 million starting from my spare room, which you can copy.

OK, before we start let's look at why you want a business in the first place ...

A Kick-Start

...something that allowed me to pay off the mortgage, to clear the credit cards and to live my life the way I choose...

In the last big recession, I lost my job. My boss came to see me and told me I was fired. At the time it was almost a relief as I hated the stress of the job, the long hours, the traffic ...

I remember the day they took back my company car and the keys to the office, together with the files I used to work on for them at home in my spare time – and I sat at home with a huge sense of relief, quite excited about the prospect of not having to go to work the next day.

> "
> **I remember, so clearly, going to the cashpoint back then and finding £10.27 as my balance – all the money I had in the entire world!**
> "

For a week it was a novelty. After a couple of weeks of waking late, without an alarm clock, drinking coffee and watching the early morning daytime TV, though, I have to admit I started to get a bit bored.

I'd walk into town and visit the Job Centre (the place I nicknamed 'The Despondency' as you'd always come out of that place feeling more depressed than when you went in). Rubbing shoulders with others who were feeling negative about life – being treated like a second-class citizen by some of the people sat behind the desks. It was the most depressing place imaginable. You could almost feel it sapping your energy as you looked through the job details to see if there was anything suitable.

It's weird but, having been employed for a few years, I had got used to the money just being in my account at the end of each month. As the bills started to mount, though, I quickly fell into panic mode as I considered how I could possibly survive with no income – and no sign of a new job on the horizon.

Things got bad. I had to move out of my nice detached house that I'd taken on when I was employed. I found myself living in a little two-up two-down rented terraced house in the rough part of town (at the end of the road was an area known locally as 'Crack Alley' for the drug abuse that went on there). I remember, so clearly, going to the cashpoint back then and finding £10.27 as my balance – all the money I had in the entire world! I sheepishly drew out my last ten pounds and, by the end of that month, found myself living on a box of Rice Krispies for a whole week. It was a very bad time.

But how could this have come about? I'd worked so hard for my employers. I was always one of the first in the office in the morning – and the last to leave at night. I'd worked weekends and evenings too – all for no additional reward. It wasn't just my time, either, that I'd given to the job. I'd put my heart and soul into it. Yet none of that mattered when it came right down to it. Out of the blue, I was 'let go'.

If you're employed at the moment ask yourself – **REALLY** – how long could you last financially if you lost your job tomorrow? How long before the money runs out and you can't pay the bills? How long before the car loan can't be paid and you have to hand the car back? How long before the mortgage payments overwhelm you and the house has to be sold?

I read a survey recently, which said that over half the population in the UK who have full time jobs are spending every penny they earn and are unable to put anything aside as a safety net.

In another recent survey, people were asked how long they could last financially if they lost their job. Most said they could only last three months. Which is fine if things are going well and there are plenty of jobs around. But, as I found back in the last recession, when jobs are scarce that three months passes very, very quickly.

As an employee I had grown used to having a feeling of safety and security – not least because my house was going up in value every year and I knew that, if I ever had to, I could always cash out the ever-increasing equity, to cover any unforeseen financial problems if I ever fell on hard times. But when I needed it most, during that recession, the market had actually fallen … house prices had dropped badly and the market had almost ground to a halt. So the safety net that I had built up on paper wasn't there … just at the time I desperately needed it. It was an illusion. It didn't exist. It was a real wake-up call for me. The whole game had changed.

When I eventually managed to get another job (there were over 300 applicants for that one job!), I knuckled down to work hard for the new company, just so that I could hang on to the wage it would bring, to pay my bills – but at the same time I swore to myself that I would never again put myself in a position where someone somewhere could say to me 'You're fired!' and put my family's finances in jeopardy. I swore to myself that I would get myself a **Plan B** – a backup … something I could run alongside my day job, to make sure I was financially secure … and which would eventually allow me to escape the madness of the 'System' and say goodbye to working for someone else, for good.

That's what I stumbled across a few years later – something that enabled me to break free … something that allowed me to pay off the mortgage, to clear the credit cards and to live my life the way I choose – and that's what this book is all about.

Actually, this is probably a good time to tell you what this book is (and what it's definitely not); what it'll show you and what I hope you'll get from it.

When I started my search for a Plan B, I sought out someone who had already done what I wanted to do. I then did everything I could to get the guy to teach me how to copy what he did. I took what I learned and set up a business in my spare room at home. All the time in the background I had this mentor figure to help me.

I've already mentioned how I flew, at short notice, to see him talking at a seminar in the USA. I'd actually come across him a few years earlier when I bought an old recording of him speaking at a similar event. But, back then, I'd never followed it up. I'd stuck with my job and career and, I guess it's fair to say, merely dreamed that *one day* I'd be doing something similar. I put that recording on a shelf and there it stayed until I had to sell my house.

It was only years later, when I was looking for my Plan B, that I dusted off that old recording and played it. I couldn't believe that all this time, sat on a shelf and later in a box in my loft, had been this guy showing me what he did to make over $30,000 a month in his spare time ... that I'd had this sat in my house and had done nothing with it for so long.

Again, gut instinct kicked in. I went online and searched for his name. As luck would have it, he had put a website together a few weeks earlier to talk about some of his methods.

With some trepidation, I emailed him, explaining that I'd had his old recording for a few years and asking if he had any up-to-date training I could follow.

He replied that he didn't – but that he was a guest speaker at an event next week and he'd put me in touch with the seminar organiser to see if there were seats available.

As I've already mentioned, within a couple of days I got an email back from the organisers offering me a seat – if I could fly out that same weekend. The rest you know.

After the event – having come back to the UK and started my own little business – I then followed this guy as much as I could. To keep me totally immersed in his way of starting and running a business I subscribed to his monthly newsletter, I bought his books, courses and DVDs ... almost anything

I could get my hands on so that I could learn as much as possible and copy what he did.

You see, I figured that if I was to make a success of this business, I needed to follow very firmly in the footsteps of the guy who had gone before me. If someone has actually come up with something, made all the mistakes and succeeded, it makes sense to learn from him/her and, hopefully, to benefit from their experiences and avoid the mistakes, right?

That's what I wanted to do for you with this book – to show you what has worked for me, so that you can copy some of these ideas for yourself – if and when you start your own business.

Will this book make you a millionaire? As I mentioned in Chapter 1, I have no way of telling, as I don't know you or what you will do with the information in the book. But doesn't it make sense to stack the deck in your favour as much as possible – by copying the ordinary bloke who banked over £50 million starting from his spare room?

This book is the equivalent of me going to that seminar 15 years ago, to hear this guy talking on stage and sharing the ways he made money at home.

I didn't expect to learn every single thing he did, in the time he had on stage – just as it would be impossible to lay absolutely every single little minute detail of my business out in this short book. But I learned enough from what I saw on stage back then to get me thinking … to give me some great ideas I could copy … and to get me started.

> **That's what this book will do for you. It'll give you a kick-start. I'll show you what I do – explain the basics of the business so you'll know not just what works, but also what to avoid.**

After attending that seminar back then, it took me a couple of years to really hit it big – to make some serious money. I had a lot to learn and a lot to work out for myself as I tried to adapt the system for the UK. But his stage presentation got me started and pointed me in the right direction.

It provided me with a good grounding … got me into the right way of thinking and gave me an outline of his business model to work to. In a nutshell, it gave me a kick-start.

That's what this book will do for you. It'll give you a kick-start. I'll show you what I do – explain the basics of the business so you'll know not just what works, but also what to avoid. (As I'll explain later, the choices you make now when deciding what type of business to start can literally be the difference between success and failure. Start off with the wrong business model and you'll be doomed to failure no matter how much time and effort you put into it. But start with a business model that's been proven to work – and you have a much greater chance of succeeding.)

As I mentioned, if you're looking for a book full of charts and projections – you've got the wrong book. If you've just finished at university and come out with a master's in Business Administration and an attitude that you know everything – this book is going to surprise you.

I held one of my training workshops a few years ago and taught everyone in that room how to start their business.

A few months later one of the attendees – who can best be described as 'a corporate man' – sent me a huge bundle of documents he had prepared and printed off, presented in a lovely, bound business-plan folder. He had carefully laid out a month-by-month breakdown of costs, sales, etc. He'd done a **SWOT** analysis (which, apparently, the business books tell you to do – to allow you to 'identify **S**trengths, **W**eaknesses, **O**pportunities and **T**hreats involved in a project or in a business venture'). He had carried out detailed assessments of market potential and come up with all manner of clever-looking nonsense that they teach you at business school. He never actually got around to starting the business. He'd clearly spent so much time in corporate la-la land, completing market appraisals and forecasts, that when faced with a simple-to-follow business model he couldn't cope.

Another of the attendees at that workshop didn't do any of that. He didn't do a forecast, or a detailed business plan. He sat in that training room and scribbled notes down as I spoke – writing down everything he needed to know, to enable him to go home that day and get his business started. Rather than sit in his spare room at his DIY desk (that he'd built himself, out of an old door), writing loads of reports and business plans with pretty-looking charts and forecasts – he just got straight down to business. He copied my system exactly as I'd shown him and, using a simple product idea I'd given him at the workshop, he ran a little ad in one of the national newspapers. That was about 12 years ago. He just followed exactly what I taught him … he copied my system. The last time I spoke to him, he'd banked over £10 million and counting.

So, if you're someone that likes to draw graphs and charts and put hugely detailed business plans together, this probably isn't going to be the right book for you. But if you want to copy a simple business idea that has seen me bank over £50 million starting from my spare room at home … and has helped other successful students of mine pull in over £1 million each, you'll probably want to grab a pen or pencil to draw some light bulbs in the margins of this book as we go through the next few chapters.

OK, let's get started …

Stack the Deck
in Your Favour

I don't like to gamble. I like to bet on a sure thing

I read somewhere that around 80% of new, traditional businesses (i.e. shops, manufacturing businesses, etc.) FAIL in the first three years. Why? Primarily because of the things I spoke about earlier when discussing my Dad and how he set up his shop. You take on huge overheads and carry a lot of costs, *before* you even know if the thing is going to work – and your profit margins tend to be very low too.

On the other hand, I also recall reading that 85% of home-based businesses **SUCCEED** – and a lot of that success has to do with keeping costs low and doing everything on a shoestring.

Now I'm not a betting man – but if you had to put your money on one type of business or another, wouldn't it make sense to choose the one with the highest likelihood of success?

The seminar that I went to – that got me started – happened to be held in Las Vegas, which is known not only as a great conference destination but also, of course, for its gambling. I have to admit I was in awe as I walked into the glamorous atmosphere of the casinos there and saw all the action and excitement as people placed their bets or were dealt a hand of cards, holding their breath to see if they had won a huge jackpot, if Lady Luck had smiled on them that day.

Most go home disappointed, because the odds are against them. You see, the casinos know with absolute certainty the odds of the punter winning a hand of blackjack or getting a winning number on roulette. And the odds are not good for the player. Yet still people queue up to try to win – and put down their hard-earned money. It's the same with business. People still queue up to open their own shop – even though the odds of success are stacked against them. They put down their cash and wait for Lady Luck.

The odds are stacked heavily in favour of the casino operator.

That's what I wanted in my business – I wanted the odds stacked in my favour. I didn't want to start a business that statistically had an 85% chance of failure before I'd even opened the door. I wanted the type of business that had a high chance of success.

When I started out I made sure I **stacked the deck in my favour** by having the following fundamentals in place.

Low start-up costs

I saw a couple on TV recently who had started their own hairdressing salon as they had always wanted 'to be their own boss'. Just to open the salon they went into debt to the tune of £350,000 for the lease, the shop fitting, builders, decorators, salon chairs, fixtures, fittings, equipment, liability insurance, etc. And that was before they had cut a single strand of hair! Their beautifully presented business plan (the modern-day equivalent of the gypsy's crystal ball!) showed £1250 profit per week as soon as the business was opened. But as the programme showed, revenues were *far* below their expectations. Imagine the horror of going into debt by £350,000 to start a business that turned out not to be profitable! Even if it had performed as predicted, the pay-back period for the start-up costs alone was *six years*! Think about that! Six years of cutting hair and … financially you have just broken even. Insane.

When I was looking for a business that I could start myself, I didn't have hundreds of thousands of pounds to invest. I'd been an ordinary 'wage slave', so there was no way I could stump up a lot of cash. I couldn't afford to take on staff, or rent premises. I didn't have the money to buy an existing business or to buy into one of those large franchises. I also didn't want to get myself heavily into debt before I knew whether the business would even work or not. No way was I going to remortgage my house or pile up the credit card debt. Neither did I want to go off and try to find investors to put their money into my new business, and have to give away a huge percentage of the business. I wanted (needed!) something I could start on a shoestring budget.

Low overheads

I mentioned in Chapter 1 that my Dad ran a hardware shop and that all through his business life he never made any money to speak of – barely surviving day to day as the retail shop model was so flawed from the outset.

Dad rented a former motorcycle shop that had become vacant at the bottom of the town. Instantly, he had taken on a large overhead – the rent for the shop. Of course it didn't stop there. He had a large business rates bill to pay to the local authority – just for the pleasure of using the shop he was now renting and responsible for.

The moment he opened for business, he started to run up a large electricity bill for lighting and he had a rental payment to make for the cash register that stood on the shop counter.

The products my Dad sold included things like large paving slabs, bags of coal, containers of bottled gas and other heavy items. His customers expected them to be delivered to their homes, so Dad had to run a delivery van too. Again, the moment he opened his business, he had a loan to repay for his van, plus road tax, fuel, tyres and repairs.

When the business took off a little, he employed a driver … yet more overheads!

As you'll see throughout this book, not only did I learn a lot from my business mentor, I also learned a lot from watching my Dad struggle in business. **I learned what NOT to do**.

The business model I wanted was one where I had **LOW overheads**.

That's what I set up. I started my business in my spare room at home. I had an old, second-hand desk I'd managed to get hold of for nothing. I had a pre-Pentium computer that took for ever to start – and one of those old 'clackety clack' printers that I always felt would wake the neighbours when

I was working late in the evening to get my business up and running.

So, you don't need the very latest computer or technology. Nor, in fact, do you need to be a techie either. When I started my business I could just about type an email, use MS Word and browse the web. That's about the skill level you need to get you started in this business.

I didn't need any staff. I didn't need any fancy office furniture. I did everything on a shoestring.

I used to pack boxes in my garage. People would phone from time to time and probably thought they were speaking to an employee of a large company. If only they could have seen the £3.99 extension cable I bought at B&Q, slung out of my spare bedroom window and trailed across the garage roof, under the eaves, to an old phone that stood on an upturned cardboard box in the corner, to provide an extension handset in the garage while the box packing was in full swing.

That's the beauty of this type of business. You can present yourself as a proper business from day one – even if you are sat at your PC or laptop in your underwear eating a late breakfast. No one can tell whether the website they are looking at belongs to a large corporation or a bloke working out of his spare room.

Unlike my dear old Dad, I didn't need to rent a shop for my customers to visit and to display my products. I only needed a simple website. The rest I could do from home. I didn't need a van to deliver the products to customers – I use Parcelforce or UKMail, or one of the other carriers.

I didn't need staff. When my business got to around 200 orders a day, I was able to outsource all of the packing and despatch work to a fulfilment house that could take care of everything, and who took a small % of the order value as a fee. If no sales came in, I didn't have to pay them either. Whereas, in Dad's shop, if he had no goods to deliver the driver still had to be paid.

> **I didn't need any staff. I didn't need any fancy office furniture. I did everything on a shoestring.**

Actually, fulfilment houses are one of the most useful resources I have ever come across. These are professional companies who will store your products on their shelves; they will answer the phone in your company name; take orders and deal with any customer order queries, refunds, etc. When an order arrives, they make up the package from your stored stock, put in a cover letter or any other paperwork, attach an address label and arrange for it to be delivered to the customer. The advantage of doing business this way is obvious: you can run your business from home – or even from your local coffee shop, just like one of my students does. Almost anywhere you can get an Internet connection, you can do business because the day-to-day 'back-room' stuff – the order processing, etc. – is all outsourced to a fulfilment house.

Low marketing costs

When I was starting out I didn't have loads of money to pay for advertising and marketing. I couldn't call a top London ad agency and ask them to create some lovely ads and book some TV airtime, or some double-page spreads in the Sunday glossies. Not that I'd want to – but that's a whole different story, which I'll get to in Chapter 7.

Again, I wanted to start my little business on a shoestring. What I did back then was to place a tiny, semi-display ad in the classifieds section of one of the Sunday papers. A simple little ad on four or five lines of text and a telephone number (which went to my answerphone) plus a website address. On the website, which was a simple one-page site and an order form, visitors could see more details of my product and order. If instead they called the answerphone, they could leave their name and address and I would send them a printed copy of what was on the website, plus an order form they could fill in and return to me in a Freepost envelope.

Now this was back before Google arrived to dominate the planet. That was the day when things got really exciting.

No longer did you have to rely just on ads in newspapers: you could also place ads on Google – those ads that appear at the top of the page and down the right hand side, that get displayed when someone types in a keyword related to your market. So, for example, if you are selling a 'How to Play Guitar' DVD, you can run simple clickable text ads on Google that will be displayed whenever anyone types in that particular phrase – or any other related phrase you care to list.

You can start on a minuscule budget and be up and running almost immediately. And the beauty is that **you only pay when someone clicks the ad to go to your website** (hence 'pay-per-click').

Whether I'm using ads in newspapers as I did back then, or pay-per-click ads on Google to make my sales – whatever the source, I then reinvest the profits generated from one ad into booking another ad or a series of ads.

Now I don't like to gamble. I like to bet on a sure thing.

So, when I wrote an ad and tested it one week – and it pulled a good response – I was then fairly safe in placing the same ad the following week in the same paper. And, of course, once I had the wording right for an ad and had tested it in one newspaper, I then tested that same ad in another paper the following week too. By constantly testing, instead of blowing all my cash on a hunch, I was able to gradually roll out my ad for maximum coverage.

Talk about **stacking the deck in your favour!** It's a bit like getting a winning hand of cards at the casino and then knowing that the next hand will win too – and the next – and the next.

> "
> Talk about **stacking the deck in your favour!** It's a bit like getting a winning hand of cards at the casino and then knowing that the next hand will win too – and the next – and the next.
> "

It's the same with pay-per-click ads. I'll test one particular set of keywords – such as *'How to Play Guitar'* and then once I am sure that is working, I'll keep that one going, bringing in the cash almost on autopilot, while I also test another set of keywords too – for example *'guitar lessons'*.

Similarly, once I have a winning ad, I'll keep that running but I'll also run a slightly differently worded version of that ad too. It might just be that the new wording pulls a better response than the original ad. It's the only way to know which wording will work best. Let the customers tell you. You can do what's called 'split testing'. You run two differently worded ads. The first person searching for *'How to Play Guitar'* sees one version of your ad. The second person searching sees your alternative ad version. The third sees the original one again – and so on. And the beauty is that this can all be done automatically for you. You then get a simple report that tells you which ad got clicked most – and, of course, which one sold most too. Guess which ad you'll use from then on?

Free publicity

Another great boost that my little business got was when I discovered what I call 'free publicity'. I wrote out an article about my first product and sent it, with some photos, to a national magazine that was aimed at my particular niche market.

To my surprise, the magazine printed every single word I had written, in their next edition. I'd included my website and my telephone number in the article – and that got printed too. So here I was – working from home – with a double-page spread in a national magazine talking about how wonderful my product was, alongside a recommendation that readers should buy it! **Remember – I'd written every word and just sent it in!** They then printed it word for word. I couldn't believe it. (Of course, now I know how the business works, when I'm scanning through the newspapers and magazines, I see loads of pieces that are actually 'donated' press releases from companies and organisations simply reworked or printed just as they were written.)

In my case, the magazine had printed my details at the foot of the piece too, so its readers could order my product online or over the phone. I had to get someone to come in to answer the phone for me that week. It was ringing off the hook!

Similarly, someone did a review of my product in his newsletter, which again was targeted at my niche market. This was a

well-respected newsletter editor writing a full-blown review –
which praised my product and gave it ten out of ten for value
for money. I was inundated with orders again. Now, in his
case, he had actually ordered a retail copy of my product from
my website, tried it out and reviewed it. You could of course
simply send complimentary copies of the product to relevant
publications for review. However, be aware that this may not
always go your way. If the reviewer doesn't like the product
for some reason, you'll still get written about. So, you may
want to play safe and send your own review article just as I
did in the first example.

The thing to remember here is that all of the orders that came
in from those **FREE publicity** pieces didn't cost me anything. If
I'd bought that double-page spread in the national magazine
for a glossy ad, it could have cost me tens of thousands – yet
I got exactly the same space for **FREE**.

I guess it's easy to understand why. If you stand back and look
at the magazine business for a second – in simple terms, they
sell as many pages of glossy ads as they can – for thousands
of pounds a page. That's where they make their big money.
Although it's a bit of a chore, they then have to put a little
'content' between the ad pages so their readers feel they are
getting something other than a glossy publication full of ads.
So they need articles. Now they can get journalists and writers
to provide these – but of course that costs them money. So, if
someone sends them a ready-made article they can use – or
even something they can rewrite and rework, to provide a

good content page – then it's an attractive thing for them to have.

I've used this same free publicity technique to get pages upon pages of coverage for nothing. On one promotion, I managed to get the equivalent of £127,000 worth of ad space – for nought. So if I'd had a big city ad agency working for me – and if I'd had the money available – I could have spent £127,000 on running some ads in a number of national papers and mags … OR I could send out some simple articles that the mags could use and get the space for FREE!

My experience is that, as long as the article is newsworthy and NOT just a blatant 'I've got this great product – you should buy it' sales piece, you'll have a good chance of it getting published.

Direct response marketing

So, I used free publicity to keep the costs of my marketing as low as possible. As the business grew I then reinvested some of the profits into dabbling with direct response marketing methods – such as direct mail.

Now, before you shout about direct mail being a bit 'old school' in this Internet age, I can tell you that of all the methods I use right now, today, direct mail is THE most responsive of all marketing methods. In my business it beats pay-per-click ads, beats email marketing, beats any form of social media marketing.

The beauty of direct mail, pay-per-click ads, classified ads, etc., is that they can all be tracked. You place an ad and you know <u>exactly</u> how many sales come from spending that little amount of money on that particular ad. You send out a letter in the post to 100 people, and you know how many sales – **EXACTLY** – came from the mailing of those 100 letters.

If I was running a business where we advertised using paid-for glossy magazine double-page spreads at £10,000+ a pop – I'd want to know exactly how many sales that £10,000 ad made. But next time you are looking through the Sunday glossies, take a look at those ads. See how many of them have a response mechanism in them that will track sales back to that specific ad.

Contrast that to a letter I send that takes people to a particular website. If I send that one letter to one specific group of potential buyers, I'll put one website address on that letter. If I send the same letter to another group, I'll send them to the same website <u>content</u> but it will have a <u>different</u> domain name. That way I can track how many sales come in from each site – so I know exactly which letters pull and which don't.

It's the same with ads, press releases, etc. If I run an ad in two different places I use different website addresses – purely so that I can track how effective each ad is. I can track every single piece of marketing I do and see which ones pull and which ones don't.

The following week I'll then advertise again in the publications that pulled – or I'll send more letters to the mailing list that pulled a decent response. Sounds pretty simple, but most big-budget corporate ads don't do this. Many large companies with huge marketing budgets spend fortunes on ads and have absolutely no idea whether they work or not.

I don't spend fortunes like that. I test out ads, letters, etc., and reinvest only in those that work. **That way I keep my marketing costs low.**

Find a hungry crowd

During one of my Masterclass workshops – which I hold to teach my system in detail, face-to-face – I asked a question of the students there. 'If each of us here started up a hot-dog stand and we held a competition to see which of us could sell the most hot dogs over a weekend, what would you focus on to make sure you won?'

I got loads of different answers – which we put up on a whiteboard. Someone said they would focus on having the best-tasting sausages. Several agreed that they would steer away for the traditional 'junk' sausage with its particularly tiny meat content and instead use only the best ingredients. One person wanted to offer vegan sausages. Someone else said they would offer different relishes and side dishes to increase profits. Someone said they would use wholemeal bread rather than those rather soggy white baps. Someone said they would check all the local fast food places and make sure that his price was lower than anyone else, to entice buyers.

We ended up with a white board full of suggestions on how to win the contest to sell most hot dogs in a weekend.

On a separate whiteboard I then wrote down the ONE thing I would want – to ensure my own success.

I wanted a **HUNGRY CROWD**

You see, you can have the greatest bread, the most amazing-tasting sausages, relishes to drool over and prices that are lower than anyone else, but if you don't have a crowd of hungry people you don't have a business.

It seems obvious, yet so many people start a business and only later consider whether anyone is likely to actually want to buy what they have.

My Dad was fond of saying 'Build a better mousetrap and the world will beat a path to your door'. Sadly for my Dad and a lot of other business owners, this is not so.

Find a group of people who are infested with mice and you can sell them *any* form of mousetrap, even a third-rate one. (I'm not suggesting you sell third-rate products, by the way.

I'm merely making the point about hungry crowds.) But find people with no mice at all and you'll be sitting in your shop for years, waiting to sell your stock of deluxe *Digital Mousetrap 2.0*. You couldn't give it away.

I'm serious here. It doesn't matter how good the design is, or even how cheap it is. If people don't have a 'mouse problem', you'll never make your fortune trying to sell them a cure.

At one of my **Entrepreneurs Bootcamp** events, a guy pulled me to one side in the lunch break and told me how he'd spent three years and over £200,000 developing a great new piece of software. He explained how it was the greatest piece of software for doing a particular task and there was nothing else like it on the market. He then asked me if I would 'do the marketing' for him – i.e. would I sell it for him, for a % of the profits.

> " In my business, to stack the deck in my favour, I look for hungry crowds of people first – people who have a particular desire – a hunger ... and only then do I look for something to sell them. "

I asked him one simple question. 'Who is it going to sell to?' He replied 'I was rather hoping you would tell me that. I've done all the work in designing it and having it made – now we just need you to sell it'.

I told him I would not be interested. I explained that he had done everything the wrong way round. He had developed a product first – without finding out if there was actually anyone that would have an interest in buying it. Taking on such a project would just be too much like hard work. I don't run my business to take on hard work. I run it to give me the **freedom** to enjoy myself.

In my business, to stack the deck in my favour, I look for hungry crowds of people first – people who have a particular desire – a hunger … and only then do I look for something to sell them.

Take one of my students as a good example. In the UK, a couple of years ago smoking was made illegal inside pubs, restaurants and other similar public places. Smoking suddenly became a more antisocial thing to do – and smokers had to stand outside in the cold and rain to puff on their tobacco.

What this meant was a huge new 'hungry crowd' of smokers in a predicament. A time when the urge to stop smoking began to rise greatly.

One of my students spotted an opportunity to market to this 'hungry crowd'. He found a 'Stop Smoking' hypnotherapy CD that he was able to licence cheaply (I'll come to licensing in a second). He sold a simple set of two CDs that he packaged up for the 'Stop Smoking' market.

Within just four weeks he had banked over £71,500 – all from spotting that 'hungry crowd' opportunity and finding something to sell them.

Following on from that he's followed the hungry crowd rule – and has so far banked over £1 million – all from a business he started in his spare room at home with a 'stop smoking' idea; all because he found the hungry crowd first – then looked for something to sell them.

Another student of mine, who came to a Masterclass workshop a few years back, saw an article in the newspaper about people in the UK buying up very cheap properties in Bulgaria as second homes. Spotting a 'hungry' market, he put together a simple 'information' product for wannabe Bulgarian second-home buyers and started a business in his spare room which went on to bank over £7 million.

If he'd sat down at his desk with a blank sheet of paper and written a list of products he'd like to sell, probably the last thing he ever would have dreamed up would have been a product showing people where and how to get cheap Bulgarian properties. Yet, through stumbling across a hungry market of people, he was pointed to an obvious first project – one that launched his multi-million-pound business.

Where to find a hungry crowd

When I'm looking for hungry crowds – as well as looking through news articles for possible ideas – I also do research in a number of other ways.

One that I have always done is to look online at mailing list broker sites. You may not know, but if, for example, someone orders a set of golf clubs from an online or mail order golf catalogue, the company selling the clubs enters their name and address onto their customer database – or 'list' as it's called in the trade.

Many such companies make money by renting their list out to other companies who have non-competing offers. (For example, a golf retailer selling to high-income professionals might rent their mailing list out to a luxury car maker, or a high-end travel company.)

Why would they do that? Because they get paid handsomely for doing so. The car maker is happy to pay money to rent the golf list, to send a luxury car brochure to each golf customer – as the golf customers are probably also in the right income bracket for luxury cars.

But how does that help us?

Well, if we go online and do a search for something like 'list broker golf' and find a list broker who has a list of **30,000 people** who bought a golfing product **in the last 12 months** – we have found ourselves a **hungry market**.

Think about it – if a guy has just bought a new set of golf clubs, does he now have everything he is ever going to spend money on, in his lifetime, for golf? Of course not. He is, in fact, likely to be in the market for not only more clubs, putters, etc., balls and tees … but he is also likely to be attracted to offers for DVDs that show how to get a hole in one, how to improve his swing, and so on. He'll also be buying the 'Rupert Bear' trousers and the shoes with the studs on … the golf bag … club memberships … one-to-one training with a golf pro … the list is almost endless!

So if we find a list broker who is offering to rent us a list of people who bought a new set of golf clubs in the last 12 months – you can see that there's money to be made.

Now this is something I couldn't get my head around when I first started. Here's a list broker who is prepared to rent me the names AND the contact details of people who have actually bought a particular golfing product in the last year, for example. I don't have to advertise. I don't have to put out press releases. This broker will send me the names and addresses of these people for as little as 15p per name/ address – and I can then send them my offer!

So as long as I can find a hungry crowd of people who have all bought something and are on a broker's list – I can sell them my products.

(By the way – golf is actually a great example, too, of people who tend to have disposable cash and will make purchases of items to improve their game. Far better to have people with cash for impulse purchases than trying to sell to a market of people who have no money to spend)

Another way I have used to find hungry crowds is to spend some time in magazine shops – WH Smith or wherever. In fact when I was just starting out, I used to get some very strange looks as I loitered in the aisles of the local newsagents. I'm sure they thought I was looking at everything on the top shelf!

But by looking along the shelves I would find clusters of magazines all on particular niche topics. Maybe 'Antique Collecting', 'Golf', 'Model Making', 'Sci-Fi', 'Building Your Own Home', 'Cross-stitch', 'Building Websites', 'Cooking', etc. etc. If there's a magazine on the shelf it is almost certainly an indication that there is a hungry crowd for the topic of the magazine. It's tough to get enough circulation to keep a magazine going, so if you see one in WH Smith, month after month, you can bet there are thousands of avid readers nationally – of 'Metal Detector News' or whatever the title is. And for each reader, there are plenty more enthusiasts who don't subscribe.

When I'm looking for a hungry market, I'll buy a few of these mags and look through the small adverts in the back. And come up with product ideas to sell the readers of that magazine.

Similarly, if I found a hot niche market on a magazine rack, I'd then go home and search online for list brokers with access to such people. Sometimes you can even get access to the subscribers list of that actual magazine too.

And remember, you don't need to know a single thing about the niche topic! The object here is *not* for you to become an expert. When I started out, I was **not an expert** at anything. I was merely the publisher. If you start this type of business, you will be a '**publisher**' too.

Another simple way to find a hungry crowd is to look online. Do a Google search for 'Google keyword tool' and you'll find a page where you can enter a phrase such as 'how to play guitar' and it will tell you how many people are searching globally on that exact term each month. At the time of writing I just checked – its 1,220,000. **1.2 MILLION people** searching for that one term … each **MONTH**! Now that's a large hungry crowd of people searching on Google (and therefore who we can advertise to cheaply using pay-per-click ads, as I briefly mentioned).

What we need to find is something to sell them …

What Sells Best – and How I Make My **Money**

"

The three things that I sell that brought in over £50 Million

"

One of the most common requests I get from students of my courses is: 'Andrew, please tell me what to sell. I don't have any products or ideas.'

Now, I have found that once I have identified a hungry crowd it is relatively easy to find products to sell. Particularly if you focus on **'How To'** products. In all the examples I gave: **How To Play Golf**; **How To Stop Smoking**; and **How To Buy Cheap Properties** ... the products sold were information products showing people how to do a particular something.

Let's quickly brainstorm a few ideas together to show you how this works.

Subjects that consistently make money

Here are ten quick ideas that you should be able to make consistent money from if you copy my system. These subjects are already making people wealthy and there's plenty of room in the market for you to join them. Pop any of these ideas into the Google keyword tool that I mentioned in the last chapter and you'll get a feel for just how many people are searching every single month for information on these topics.

The list here is not in any particular order, by the way – one is not necessarily better than any other. I'm just popping down a few ideas to give you some pointers.

Idea #1 – Money-making information
This is a huge hot topic. At the time of writing, I just checked

Google's keyword tool and it shows that **5,000,000 (five million!!) people a MONTH** are searching on the term *'make money'* while <u>a further 2.7 million are searching for 'how to earn money'</u>. Not only are there millions of potential buyers out there searching, but there are a hundred and one topics to cover too.

Here are a few suggestions, so you get the idea: make money with your camera; the Internet; renovating property; car boot and garage sales; buying and selling on eBay; organising events and parties; wedding planners; home publishing; stock market trading.

In other words, your subject is all the different ways people can make money.

Idea #2 – Money-saving information

This is never going to be as lucrative as the 'make money' idea. But, in these times of austerity, people also focus on saving money – whether it's on travel, food, hotel rooms, cars – on almost everything they do. For example, at the time of writing, over 11 million people are searching every month for information on cheap flights.

Topic ideas: choosing an energy supplier; cutting your grocery bill in half; how to get hotel rooms for less than half price; cut-price travel tips; cut-price property deals; how to live a rich lifestyle on an average income; how to get an upgrade on a flight; and how to save 30% on getting your car serviced.

Idea #3 – Any good 'how to' information

Any title that begins with 'how to' usually makes a great information product as long as you can find a hungry crowd for the information.

For instance: how to build your own house; how to dance (which at the time of writing has around **68 million people a month** searching online!); how to research your family tree; how to teach your child to read; how to make money; how to make wine and beer; how to solar heat your home; how to pole dance; how to do magic tricks …

The possible 'how to' topics list is huge. They have always been popular and they probably always will be.

Idea #4 – Health information

The health market never seems to stop expanding. Millions of people are looking for alternative ways to protect their health or to overcome illness.

Many people are disenchanted with the modern health system and are even travelling to other countries for alternative treatments, rather than attending a hospital in the UK.

Topic ideas: directory of the best hospitals across Europe; Chinese herbal remedies; shiatsu; the twelve health centres in your body; yoga; the perfect body; think yourself ten years younger; acupuncture; lower high blood pressure (there are over **6 million people a month** searching online for information about blood pressure alone!) …

Idea #5 – Weight loss and diet information

Check out January 1st – and the New Year's resolutions. How many people choose that date to change their eating habits and to try to lose weight? In most cases they will change for a few weeks at most – then fall back into old habits. So, show me a list of people who bought a diet plan or joined a gym last New Year and I'll show you how to make money next New Year when they write their brand new list of resolutions, which will include, once again, the topic of losing weight. (At the time of writing this chapter – which happens to be January – over **30 million people are searching on the term 'diet' this month!!** I'll resist the temptation to crack a joke about huge hungry markets.)

Topic ideas: 14-day weight loss course; weight loss for your wedding day; six-pack abs in 30 days; toned upper body exercises; lose X pounds in X days; the no carb, no starvation, diet; lose weight in just three minutes a day …

Idea #6 – Information for senior citizens

Most western nations are in the grip of a massive demographic time bomb. The number of senior citizens is rising dramatically, mainly because people are living longer, healthier and more active lives. This is a huge and quite wealthy marketplace, and this can relate to health, too, because as people age they become more interested in health issues.

They're also interested in getting bargains. They're interested in travel. They're interested in finding holiday spots and new places to live.

Topic ideas: holidays for the over-60s and young at heart; cut-price travel in style; 101 gift ideas for the grandchildren; 101 leisure activities; the top hotels in Europe; clubs and courses; bargain holidays; selling up and living abroad; investing wisely; equity release schemes explained.

Idea #7 – Gambling

Gambling is huge in the UK with the advent of online bingo and poker. There is also horse and dog racing. Millions of people are into gambling, whether it's good for them or not.

Topic ideas: how to beat the blackjack dealer; how to win at the dogs; how to find a genuine horse-racing tipster; how to win at Texas hold 'em poker.

Note: this isn't a market I tend to offer products to – that's just my personal choice – but you only have to watch the TV ads to know that gambling is a huge, hungry market.

Idea #8 – Dating and personal relationships

This is a big topic because there are something like 60 million single people in the United States and nearly 10 million in the UK. By the way, I mention the US here as, although most of my £50 million has come from the UK market alone, you can copy the ideas in this book to start your own business almost anywhere in the world and sell into the massive US market too if you wish. The principles are exactly the same and you'll be able to find fulfilment houses in the US to handle everything there for you, just as I do in the UK.

Topic ideas: how to have a happy marriage; how to find your soul mate; how to single out the special person in your life; how to win friends; 101 ways to get results from online dating; specialist dating agencies; 50 ways to spice up your relationship; top 20 chat-up lines …

Idea #9 – Investment information

This is always popular. (Over **four million people a month** are searching for information on 'how to invest'.) People want to know how to invest money, to make more money than they can get by putting it in the bank. This can include all sorts of topics related to stocks, shares and property as well as traditional and non-traditional investments. Obviously you have to be very careful not to break any laws preventing you from offering specific investment advice. Just keep your advice confined to general principles.

Topic ideas: how to invest in commodities; mutual funds; bonds; investing in the future; unusual investments; gold and precious metals; how to make money with forex; buying and selling property; spread-betting on financial indices …

Idea #10 – The unusual

This is anything that's unusual or bizarre. This covers a wide variety of things from survival information (do a Google search on 'how to survive'… and you'll find plenty of unusual things people are worried about and want to prepare for) to things as wild as flying saucers and alien race conspiracies.

Topic ideas: teach your dog to sing; how to photograph a ghost; how to be self-sufficient; grow your own exotic tropical vegetables; conspiracy theories; how to eat for free; how to breed piranhas; 101 uses for vinegar; keeping crocodiles; how to talk to your cat; the alien seekers UFO site guide; preparedness for when the oil runs out; etc.

OK, so that's a quick list of ten topic idea headlines for products that you could market – but how do we make money from them?

How I make my money

As I've said I am a '**Publisher**'. I publish and sell information. I am in the **information publishing** business. Now, don't worry – you don't have to write or create anything yourself to sell. Someone else does that for you, as I'll show you in Chapter 5. In the same way that a book publisher doesn't write all the books they publish, I don't create the products that I publish either. I simply line up 'hungry' customers and deliver other people's products (**information**) to them.

I deliver (sell!) this **information** in three main formats:

1 **Paper products** – newsletters, manuals, courses and books.

2 **Digital products** – audio CDs, DVDs, digital products.

3 **Live events** – workshops and seminars.

All have the same theme – **information** delivered in one form or another.

So, for example, if I decide to get into the weight-loss niche, I could sell books and manuals on a particular diet or exercise plan – or maybe a monthly subscription newsletter with different dieting tips, recipes, exercises, etc. I can also offer DVDs showing a personal trainer teaching exercise techniques. I could market an app or some audio files to help with a training regime or a diet plan. I could also hold live events – maybe a weight-loss boot-camp weekend retreat, or weekly diet meetings. All of these deliver information to the target market and all meet the strict criteria I have for the types of products I will sell – i.e. the three types listed above.

> **Now, don't worry – you don't have to write or create anything yourself to sell. Someone else does that for you, as I'll show you in Chapter 5.**

I get loads of people coming to me asking if I will sell their new widget – but I always turn down such offers as they don't fall within my highly profitable product format list.

You see, I don't want to have to import a container load of widgets, pay for them and put them in a warehouse, before I even know if they will sell. And what if I only sell half of them – I'm left with loads of stock that won't sell – and that's probably most of my profits tied up there, ready to go in a skip.

In my business, if a customer sends me an order (<u>with his/ her money</u>!!) for a CD or a booklet, I can run off a copy and send it in the post that same day. Job done. No stocks left over – no money tied up. Just good positive cash flow. It's a great business to be in – as you'll see as I explain further in the next few chapters.

The good news is that you can copy this idea for yourself.

OK, so what are the benefits of selling information products?

Let's start with money. This system has enabled me to semi-retire on a £1,000,000-per-year income 'working' just a few hours a week.

It's also something which has made a dramatic difference to the people I've taught this to … people who have taken action, copied the idea successfully and gone on to get spectacular results.

For instance, one lady and her partner, who had struggled with a little information product they were trying to sell, came to me asking if my system could be used to turn their info product into a profitable project. I worked with them to help them create a one-day live event – a training workshop – at which they would provide their information to people face to face, rather than on a DVD. I also helped them to put together a manual and a CD-ROM resource disc for the attendees.

We booked a meeting room at a local hotel and invited people along. When we knew how many people were attending, we then simply ran off the relevant number of CDs and manuals. In this way there tends to be no wasted stock in our business.

> **Within a year of applying my system, their simple project, which they had been struggling to sell and make money from, had made a massive profit of over £2,000,000.**

Within a year of applying my system, their simple project, which they had been struggling to sell and make money from, had made a massive profit of **over £2,000,000**. Yet all they were selling was information, using the three high-profit product types I recommended. A live event plus a CD-ROM and a paper workbook.

When you see what's involved, I'm sure you'll understand how quickly this system can make money once it's set up properly.

Amazingly, this can even be achieved with no product of your own. When I started I had no product of my own – I sold someone else's product (I'll explain this as we work through the following pages) yet I managed to bank my first million.

By the way, if I was put on a yacht in the Caribbean with nothing but Internet access and my laptop – and set the challenge of making a quick hundred thousand pounds, starting with a shoestring budget and with no product of my own – the techniques you'll read about here are the very ones I would use.

And I'd be 100% confident of success because I've done this kind of thing many times over in the past few years.

I recall one time, a couple of years back, when I was relaxing and sunning myself for a month on a private island. By the time I returned to the UK, my bank balance had grown by some £316,875 despite being thousands of miles away and despite the fact that I had been doing almost no work! I set the system up almost on autopilot before I left and did nothing else except check a few emails each day on my laptop.

To give you other examples you may be interested to know …

- In one year alone the system I use pulled in over £3.5 million pounds.

- On one occasion I used the same system to generate the profits to allow me to pay cash for my £1,000,000 house in Surrey – something that took only a short time to achieve.

- I then used the system again to buy a £1,000,000+ beachfront property – again for cash.

That's what selling information products has done for me.

One of the major benefits of selling information products is that there are no pre-set values for your product. For example, if I go into a book store to buy a paperback book, I know within reason that the price is going to be in the region of £9.99 to £19.99 – depending on the subject.

Similarly, if I go online and buy a DVD from the major retailers – maybe a Hollywood blockbuster – I expect to pay about £10–12. Prospective buyers have a pre-conceived idea of what a Hollywood DVD will cost them.

But information that they can't get anywhere else – that just happens to be provided to them on DVD – that's a whole different ball game.

I have personally sold sets of DVDs containing information that is not available anywhere else – for high-ticket values. For example, I sold a set of 50 DVDs (which cost me about 54 pence each to produce) for over £1500!

To the buyer that was the best £1500 he or she had ever spent as it provided them with something they desperately needed and wanted – and were prepared to pay a lot of money for.

Yet, if you followed the High Street pricing norm of £10 for a DVD, I would only have received a third of what I actually got paid.

So, selling information means you can pretty much set your own prices – if you have something someone wants.

A simple example: if I offer to sell you a sheet of paper, what would you pay me for it? A penny maybe – two perhaps?

But if that piece of paper contained the winning numbers for next week's lottery – a lottery that has a jackpot estimated at £20 million – what is that single piece of paper worth to you now? £1 million? … £10 million? … more?

It's the information on the paper that is worth the money – not the actual sheet of paper itself. Information has value and the scarcer that information is, the higher the price.

So, in the case of the lady and her business partner, which I mentioned a couple of pages ago, they had some amazing information that they were trying to sell for around £497. They thought they had reached the peak of the price they could charge.

But I showed them how to package **the same information** and deliver it at a face-to-face workshop instead (the third product type from my list, you'll recall). They sold the **SAME** information that they were trying to sell for £497 – but this time, with my help – for **£2997**! Adding around **£2500 EXTRA profit** to each sale they made.

People were prepared to pay a lot to learn what these two knew. They simply used my system to pull in **£2,000,000 profit** that year … and it's a system you could copy too.

A sample project idea

Let's look at a sample project together to see how this might work. How about, for example, those 'building your own home' magazines?

What's the one thing that prospective home builders are going to need?

Certainly, in the UK, the one scarce resource for self-builders is available building land.

Could you find a source of details of all available building plots on the market? Sure you could with a few hours' research! Could you put together a monthly subscription newsletter with these details, publishing the latest building plots to come on the market? That would tick the box for you publishing a paper product.

Do you think a simple little classified advert in the self-build type magazines would get some subscribers? Oh yes! A mere 1000 subscribers at just £19.95 a month would bring you around **fifteen grand a month profit**. And 1000 subscribers is nothing. I have published subscription products with upwards of **30,000 subscribers**. Do you see how this works? £15k a month for cranking out a few sheets of paper which would take you, maybe, half a day? You email the PDF or Word document to your printer/mailer and they do everything else. The money comes into your account on regular standing order or repeat billing done automatically for you online.

How about coming up with other products to sell to this market?

1. **Paper products** – manuals or guides on planning law, how to get planning permission, building regulations, etc. House plans; tips and tricks; 101 disasters of home housebuilding; 10 common mistakes; 20 tips for success, etc.

2. **DVDs** – get permission from someone who is already building their own house to video the whole process from start to finish including interviews as the work is progressing. (Don't forget to include all the 'human interest' bits where they are angry or despairing. It makes good TV.) Make up a set of DVDs and sell them. Pay the self-builders a percentage if necessary, but most people are content to have a bit of fame.

3. **Digital products** – could you find a piece of software to sell that would allow the self-builder to create a spreadsheet of all of the costs, right down to the last nail, in order to work out the build cost, versus the final value of the property? Or a piece of software to create a wall-planner showing all the building stages and targeted dates for completion of each stage? Or could you get a freelancer from a site like www.elance.com to build such a piece of software for you, cheaply?

4. **Workshops** – could you get a couple of self-builders to do a talk on their experiences? Invite along suppliers of timber frame kit houses, bathroom suppliers, brick manufacturers, etc. (even get some sponsorship from some of them perhaps). You could soon fill a seminar with potential self-builders, keen to learn more about the process. People will

pay for information! You can also take a percentage of any 'back of the room' sales – and on a complete house kit, this could be thousands.

The self-build example was just off the top of my head. You'll need to research your market and spend time looking for products – but it provides a good illustration of how finding a hungry crowd first (the people who buy niche market magazines, for example) can lead to the products that those people want to buy, rather than coming up with a product first only to be disappointed when nobody wants it.

If the self-build market doesn't appeal – how about choosing another of the topics I came up with earlier? Do a Google search on 'conspiracy theory' and you'll enter a whole different world of people interested in such things. There's a conspiracy theory surrounding just about any major event you care to think of in recent history – the sinking of the *Titanic*, the Moon landings, Princess Diana's death, 9/11, the Kennedy assassination … the list is almost endless.

Could you copy my system and apply it to that particular hungry crowd of people interested in conspiracy theories? Of course …

Newsletters featuring a different conspiracy theory each month. CDs and DVDs on the topic featuring 'expert' conspiracy theory 'gurus' (look around online– you'll find loads of people with their own pet theory, who would love to be interviewed and put on DVD to explain their take on events). Having built a following with your newsletter – could you then hold a seminar where you get a number of speakers to talk on stage about their own conspiracy theories and get your subscribers to come along? Absolutely.

Find the hungry crowd first and then copy my system, applying it to that particular niche market.

Of course, when someone is 'hungry' and the only person who can provide what they want is you, they are not then scurrying around town checking out the lowest prices. There is only one way they can get the information they want – through doing business with you. And you can (within reason) set a proper price for what you have to offer. You don't need to give it away for some ridiculously low price.

Take the housebuilding idea. This is a great example, because it's likely that your customers are committed to spending a few hundred thousand or more on their project – so your step-by-step manual (at say £197) is not a lot of money for them, in relation to their project.

Could they get the information that's in your manual for themselves? Sure – after weeks of research. But why would they do that when they can save themselves the hassle and buy it from you for £197 and have it sent to them the next day?

By the way, as I've said, it is not essential that you know anything about your chosen market. You need to understand the principle of finding the hungry crowd first – then finding a product to sell them and how to stand in the middle collecting the money. Please don't try to copy the system until you really get this.

For example, I recently worked with a financial trader who taught people how to make money on the commodities markets. I knew absolutely nothing about the trading of cocoa, gold and rice, or even how those markets worked. But I did know how to market his knowledge to his hungry customers. So, working with him, applying my system, we created books (paper products), some DVDs and a two-day 'live' Commodities Trading workshop. We ticked all the boxes of my system, applied to his particular niche market. That project pulled in a large amount of money – and we each took 50% of the profits on every one of those products sold. That's the power of copying my system and applying it. Once you know how it works you can make money without having an existing product of your own – all you need to know is how to seek out hungry crowds of people and how to use the system.

But what if you are not ready to put a product together yourself? What if you don't have any special information – no product of your own that you can sell for huge profits?

That's the position I was in when I started my business in my spare room. I'd been in the housebuilding business – I had no special knowledge that people would pay lots of money for. I had no product I could sell.

But I found the answer to that problem – a solution that set me on course for my first £ million …

5

Where to Get Ready-made Products to **Sell**

This part of the system was a great revelation to me when I first figured it out. One of those moments when you punch the air and shout 'Yesss!!' at the top of your voice. This one part of the system was a game changer for me and my little start-up business.

I've already mentioned that to copy this type of business, you don't need to be an expert on a particular niche topic – you will instead be the publisher. As the publisher you don't need to know anything about the topic in question. That's someone else's speciality. Now bear in mind that your speciality is to market information in different formats, through copying the ideas in this book.

So, for example, when I started out I had no absolutely idea how to pull together the necessary information to put in a monthly newsletter or to put onto DVDs for the particular hungry crowd I had found.

And having come from a corporate job, I certainly wasn't an expert in something that thousands of people would want to pay money for.

So, I needed to find myself an **expert**, someone who had information that people would buy if it was offered to them in the right way. Think of it a bit like a book publisher wanting to publish a series like the *For Dummies* books. The book publisher isn't the expert on all of the topics covered in those books. How could they be? If you look on Amazon there are over 75 pages of *For Dummies* titles to choose from – covering everything from nutrition, to guitar playing, to cognitive behavioural therapy, to growing your own fruit and veg! There is no way one person could write all of those books as the expert.

Instead, the publisher's expertise is in putting together and marketing books. They simply get authors who <u>ARE</u> experts on fruit and veg, or guitar playing – or whatever topic – to provide the content for the books. An expert author may get paid a fee for their writing; and then it's the publisher's role to sell as many copies as they can.

It's the same in the music industry. The guy running the record label doesn't have to be able to play a single note of music or to have a singing voice. His expertise is in marketing albums and singles. He gets the artist – the expert – to provide the music to go on the albums.

My business is no different. Having identified a hungry crowd of people interested in a particular topic, I then find an existing expert who has products or materials that would be of interest to that crowd. I then approach that expert and ask if he would consider **licensing** his products to me, so that I can sell them.

Now, you might be wondering why he would do that when he could sell his products himself and keep all the money. But the reality is that an expert, say on the topic of 'conspiracy theories', probably has absolutely no idea how to market that expertise (unless he's read this book and copied the system I'm laying out here or is a student of one of my courses).

If this expert has, say, some DVDs that he has made – but no idea how to get them out to the market – he might put up a little amateurish-looking website – or worse, pay a web designer a huge fee to make him a pretty-looking website that just sits there online selling nothing. (With the greatest of respect to web designers – they also know very little about what sells, they just know how to put together lovely-looking websites. I get frustrated when students of mine send me a link to a site that they have paid a guy a lot of money to produce – which they didn't need to spend – asking why it isn't selling, and having to explain to them that they've not followed the system I've taught them. Instead they have allowed a 'techie' or a 'designer' to take control. But enough of that for now … back to products and licensing.)

The expert has gone to the expense of filming a series of DVDs on his pet topic. It's probably taken him months to do. He's edited them, put some nice titles on them, added some music, created packaging designs and made a nice boxed set of DVDs that he wants to sell – but really has no idea about how to go about marketing them. So it's possible that if someone like you or I comes along and offers to buy a non-exclusive licence to those DVDs for a sum of money – the expert who has spent his own money already putting his products together might be keen to accept.

By granting you or me a non-exclusive licence to his DVD set – he has not given away his rights to sell the set himself or to license it to anyone else as well. He's simply allocated you a licence to sell sets of the DVDs yourself – in return for which he's got some much-needed cash to help towards his filming costs, etc.

Now that sounds like something that could be complicated – but it's not. Let me give you a couple of real examples ...

When I was starting out I attended a three-day seminar and noticed that the seminar organisers had employed a camera crew to film the whole thing for them, from the back of the room. Three whole days of a live workshop-style event featuring a number of expert speakers on stage covering a particular niche subject, all recorded onto 21 master video tapes by two professional camera guys.

The morning after the event I invited the seminar organiser for breakfast before he packed up his truck and headed for home. Now, bear in mind that I had no idea what I was doing. I found myself almost bluffing my way through that breakfast.

There was no way I mentioned that I was just about to give up my job and start a business in my spare room at home. Instead, I put on a bit of a show, dressed myself well, took several deep breaths and met the guy for breakfast. We chatted about the event and gradually got around to discussing the possibility that he might like to license me the whole recording of the seminar, **in return for a small one-off fee**. Over coffee we talked about his business and how he sold almost exclusively to people in the US. He had no real interest in what he saw as a tiny market in '*little old England*'. It was a market he wasn't really tapped into. He was making enough money already from the huge population of the US – so dealing with UK sales wasn't something he bothered with.

So here across the table from him, eating New York steak and eggs with OK sauce, was a guy from the UK who reckoned he could sell copies of the seminar recording in the UK and Europe … and what's more, this English guy was willing to pay some money for a copy of all the seminar tapes, which could then be edited and put onto DVDs or whatever medium, for the British audience.

From the organiser's side it was a real no-brainer. His only cost was to run off a spare set of master tape copies (a few dollars each). Since the UK wasn't his market anyway, the whole UK thing was just additional profit from his event. In fact, looking back 15 years later, my payment to him for the licence to those tapes probably paid the cost of him getting the camera guys to record it in the first place.

This not only gave the seminar organiser some cash in return for simple copies of the master tapes – but it also got him some exposure to a brand new audience in the UK as well – which could be good for his business in future too, if he decided to start operating worldwide.

On the flip side … hmm, well there really wasn't a down side for him at all.

You could almost see the smile on his face as he haggled over the price. He probably couldn't believe his luck. Here he was – he'd just had a successful seminar and was about to head home – when some mad Englishman asked him if he would like some money in exchange for a recording of the event. So we agreed a price, which I stuck on my credit card.

Within a few weeks of my return to the UK, I had in my hands a set of the master tapes and a tape player that I managed to source. **I was in business with a ready-made product to sell**!

With the tapes came a single piece of paper. A 'Certificate of Reprint and Duplication Rights'. It had my name at the top and contained a simple list of what I could and couldn't do with the recording. I could split up the set and sell them individually; I could rename and re-title them; I could charge what I liked; **and most importantly I could sell as many copies as I liked and all of the sales proceeds were mine!** So whether I sold 10 copies or 10,000 copies, the income was all mine – **no royalties to pay, no commissions, no profit-shares**.

> " **I could charge what I liked; and most importantly I could sell as many copies as I liked and all of the sales proceeds were mine!** So whether I sold 10 copies or 10,000 copies, the income was all mine – **no royalties to pay, no commissions, no profit-shares**. "

That one licensing deal done over breakfast was the start of my £50 million business.

Similarly, I once bought a licence to a simple piece of software. It came about because I needed a piece of software for my new business, to keep all of the customer records on as each new sale was made. Up until that point I had been recording my customers' names and addresses on postcard-sized pieces of card and putting them in one of those plastic filing boxes. I found a simple piece of software that I bought and put on my PC at home. It enabled me, as a non-techie person, to keep track of my business. It was an amazingly simple piece of software to use. In fact I was so happy with it – and I'd never seen it in this country before – that I approached the owner to see if he would consider licensing me a copy so that I could sell the program myself in the UK.

Now I know absolutely nothing about software and, at the time, my techie skills were limited to word processing and email. But I knew that there were other businesses out there (a hungry crowd) who would be interested in what this software could offer them.

To my delight, the programmer who had developed it emailed me back and said he would be interested in such a deal but he would need a decent amount of money to pay for his development costs. Fearing the worst, I asked him to name a figure.

His reply ... £500!

I couldn't believe my luck. To get someone to write such a program from scratch would cost thousands – then there was the process of ironing out all the bugs, six months of beta testing etc … yet here was a ready-made piece of software that I knew worked well, as I'd been using it myself – and the guy would sell me a non-exclusive licence for a mere £500.

For my £500 I was sent a master CD containing the software, a second disc containing an instruction manual that I could print out for my customers if I wanted to – and some artwork for labels, etc.

<u>The licence entitled me to run off as many copies of the software as I wanted to and to sell as many copies as I could – and to keep all the money!</u>

Now this software sold for about £80. For that I sent my new customers a disc containing a copy of the software and an instruction manual. The manual cost me around £5 to print at the local shop and included a nice binder to put it in. The disc for the software cost me around 16p. All up, including a jiffy bag and postage, my costs to get the product to the customer were around £7. So for every copy I sold I made around £73 clear profit.

I still get a tingle when I think that I sold several thousand copies of that software over the years. Several thousand copies at £73 profit each. Yet I only had to pay a one-time fee of £500 for the licence.

But that 'tingle' is nothing compared to the next licence deal I did.

By the way, as with everything else in this book, I'm not writing about these to boast in any way or to try to make out I'm clever or some sort of genius … not at all. I am just trying to show you that this one simple part of my business model has worked time after time. In this book, I'm simply laying out what has worked successfully for me, so that you can copy these ideas and get your own business up and running quickly. In particular, here, I'm trying to show that you don't have to find tens of thousands of pounds to get a ready-made product.

For example, back when I was starting out, video tapes were the medium of choice – before DVD. I was offered a licence to a set of three video tapes on a specific niche topic. If I recall, the set was called 'Product Development for Profit' or some such similar title. Nothing glamorous. I paid around £500 for a non-exclusive licence and was sent a set of three master tapes. I sent those tapes to a duplication company in Bristol who then ran off copies for me. Later on, they remastered the set and put them onto DVDs for me as well.

I decided to sell the set of three for £49.95. Each set cost about £6 to produce including the copying, postage, packing, etc., leaving me with a profit of around £44 a set.

Over the next three years **I sold around 10,000 (ten thousand!) sets at £49.95 each**. That's around **half a million pounds** in sales, from a set of three video recordings I licensed for just £500!!

If you consider the time, money and effort that would have gone into paying an expert to sit in front of a video camera for a few days and deliver some great content – add to that the costs of hiring a camera crew to film it, the lighting, the editing, the title graphics etc. – that could have amounted to £ thousands to put together such a set. Yet here was a guy who had produced the finished video footage and was prepared to license it to me for a mere £500.

Now you can see why I get so excited about this business model … and hopefully now you can also see how a down-to-earth guy, who left school with woodwork and drawing O-levels, can go on to become a multi-millionaire in a few years by starting a publishing business from scratch in his spare room at home … and how you can copy these ideas for yourself.

These days I've gained a good reputation in the trade for being someone who is always on the lookout for licensed products – either for myself or for my private students that come to my small training workshops and who want ready-made products so they can get started right away. So I get product owners from all corners of the planet coming to me with licensing offers – product developers who put products such as books, CDs, DVDs and software together and then come to me to see if I might buy a licence.

I only do a few brand new projects each year, so a lot of these ready-made product licensing opportunities simply don't get taken up by me. If you are serious about copying my system and starting a business of your own, I'm more than happy to pass on details of any suitable product licence offers that you might be able to use.

Just go to **www.ask-andrew.com** and leave your details. I'll keep you posted on anything that comes in that might be suitable for you. (Just last week for example, I was offered a licence to a set of four DVDs – a nice boxed set aimed at a hot niche market. The guy only wanted around £200 for the worldwide licence – on a product that would probably sell for around £49.95 a set.) Leave your details at **www.ask-andrew.com** and I'll pass on anything similar that comes in.

Adding the Secret Sauce

I'm sure by now you'll be thinking – 'Hmm – you pay £500 and sell half a million pounds worth … it can't be that simple or everyone would be doing it!'

As I developed my business, I tried things out – some worked, others didn't. The beauty of studying my system – through this book and my courses – is that you get to learn what works without jumping over all those hurdles I encountered when I was experimenting in the early days, just to see what worked.

Let me share something that I only normally share with students of my monthly *Cash On Demand* course. It's the difference between paying £500 for a licence and making little or no money with it – or pulling in that £half a million from the same product. Like everything in this book, it's not theory. It's based on what works for me every time …

If you look online for product licences, you may find some that are realistically priced. Most of the offers you'll find come with ready-made website pages, ready-made labels and DVD case graphics … and most sites explain how all you have to do is pop those ready-made web pages up online and wait for the cash to tumble in. Great idea, right? A ready-made website … AND ready-made packaging labels. **WRONG!**

Let's look at the example of the set of three videos I mentioned earlier – of which I sold 10,000 sets.

Now the product developer who put that three-video set together originally, also supplied ready-made website pages and packaging, labels, etc., as part of the licensing package.

He then offered licences on the open market to anyone willing to pay him £500. Loads of people bought the package. Loads of people loaded up the ready-made website pages … and then sat by their PCs waiting for the money to roll in.

But think about that for a second. If a potential buyer looked online for the product – what would they find? Loads of websites all looking exactly the same (I mean **EXACTLY** the same – same pictures, same graphics, same wording, same title, same offer, same picture of the product, same 'order now' button, same copyright details. A whole lot of online clones of exactly the same website offering exactly the same product. The problem with that high level of competition is that no one makes much money. There's no way to stand out from all the others. You just have to hope that some buyers happen to land on your particular website and buy the product from you, rather than anyone else's cloned site. But with hundreds of identical sites out there, it's a matter of pure luck. You put your site up there online and wait for Lady Luck to come up with a sale. That's no better than my Dad waiting in his shop hoping that someone will wander in and buy something. Your website could be sat there for years trying to get sales.

In fact I recently checked and found that, even now several years down the line, there are still copies of that same cloned website online – still trying to sell the same old offer.

If you copy what I'm going to share right now, you'll never be in that position.

Now I talked to a few people who bought those licences and used the ready-made cloned website to promote the product. Bottom line – they didn't make many sales.

In fact, you could almost see tears in the eyes of one guy, when I told him I had sold over **10,000 sets**. He'd sold less than 10.

But we both bought the **same** product licence – we both had the same raw materials – the masters of the recording, the ready-made website pages, the packaging, etc. All sent to each of us in a nice box along with a certificate that said **we could sell as many copies as we liked, worldwide and keep all the money**. So how come one guy sold 10 and one guy sold 10,000? What was it that made the difference of 9990 sales?

You'll want to draw a huge light bulb in the margin here. Copy this idea and you'll leave behind all the other people who buy a licence to the same product as you. Grab a highlighter and highlight this next word …

Rebranding

When I was figuring out how to make my fortune in this business, I came to the realisation that if there are 100 people worldwide who buy a licence to a particular product – and that product licence comes with ready-made website pages, sales material, etc. – you'll end up with 100 websites out there on the Internet, all looking the same: with the same words and the same product shots. I swiftly came to the conclusion that I would have less chance of making any money due to the amount of competition.

> **You'll want to draw a huge light bulb in the margin here. Copy this idea and you'll leave behind all the other people who buy a licence to the same product as you.**

Another huge issue when there is a lot of competition is that people start offering discounts and reduce their prices. It's a natural thing to do. If there are 100 identical websites all offering the same product, the only thing likely to get you the sale rather than one of the other 99 sites is price.

I could see that, if a price war broke out, some idiot would end up offering the product for an insanely small amount of money and that would be the end of the opportunity to make money from the licence I had bought.

So I needed to do something to make <u>my</u> offer stand out from the crowd, to make my product look totally different to the others out there – where the licensee had simply taken the lazy route and used the cloned, ready-made website materials to market the product.

The first thing I did was to change the title of the product. (Check the licence that comes with the product to make sure that you are allowed to do this. Almost all licences I ever negotiate have to include this in the terms, or I'm not interested.)

Imagine you buy a licence to a product called 'Golf Secrets'. Maybe you could change the title on the DVD boxes and the labels to 'How to Get a Hole in One!' Instantly you have 99 sites selling 'Golf Secrets' and only one site – yours – selling 'How to Get a Hole in One!'

In my monthly *Cash On Demand* course, I teach my students an easy way to create new covers for DVD boxes themselves – or how to get a DVD duplication house to do the work for you (**www.cash-on-demand-course.com**). It's a simple enough job – and worth doing bearing in mind the £ half a million example I mentioned a moment ago!

Having come up with a good, solid, professional-looking DVD cover and label, I then just get a freelance web guy to rework the website for me too. Now that's not as difficult as it sounds. The sales copy (i.e. the written offer on the website) simply needs to be totally different to the text on the other, 'clone' websites that the lazy guys are using.

To make my offer stand out, I normally write a different headline to start with – to grab the reader's attention. It is reckoned that you have less than 3 seconds to grab someone's attention on a first visit – otherwise they click and go somewhere else. So, the first thing they see on their screen had better reach out and grab them, and then hang onto them while they read on through your offer. To do that, I simply write out the offer in a different way. I look for a different angle – one that the ready-made websites do not offer.

(By the way – you don't need to be a good writer to do this. If you can follow a simple recipe I can show you how to write this offer out.)

> **Now in this book there isn't room to teach you everything, as I mentioned. The book is to show you a business model you can copy. If you want to learn how to write the web page offer out in a compelling way that will keep their attention, my monthly Cash On Demand course shows you, in detail, how to do that.**
>
> **Go to www.cash-on-demand-course.com and I'll send you a free month's trial and some DVDs with my compliments.**

As a good example of reworking the written offer – if we look at the video product that sold 10,000 copies, mentioned earlier, you'll see where I am coming from. The title of the set was originally something like *'Product Development for Profit'*. Now that's a very boring title anyway – but the fact that others had the same licence meant that I needed to come up with a different angle altogether.

The footage itself featured a guy living in a small rural town in the backwoods of Arkansas, who made money with a simple video camera and who worked from home, making video products to sell.

First – as with all the products I license – I watched the footage over a few times and made some notes. I then came up with a brand new title for the set of *'How To Make £30,000+ A Month From Home'*. Now that's a product title that would grab anyone's attention. I then took that title and rewrote the website – explaining what a purchaser would get from watching the recording.

Having rewritten the text for the website, I then got a freelancer to make me a brand new web page (you can get this done at **www.elance.com** very cheaply). I asked him to make it look totally different to the ready-made one – and to include pictures of the newly named product set that I had created. By the way, the type of website I use to sell such a product is only two pages. Nothing clever or fancy. It has a main home page containing the offer itself and an order form page. That's it. That's all you need.

So I went from having a standard-looking website that everyone and his dog also had – attempting to sell the same product with the same mundane title – to a totally unique website that I owned, that had a totally new look and fresh feel to it … that showcased a professional-looking package of products … that was now totally different to anyone else's offering.

It's a technique I have since used year after year whenever I decide to license someone else's ready-made product.

It's just one of the techniques I use in my business to stack the deck heavily in my favour.

But there's something else I do that almost guarantees me profits …

6

How to Go from Making a Few Hundred Pounds... to Banking Your **First Million**

"

...the difference between you starting a mediocre business that earns you a living, or having a business model with the potential to make you an awful lot of money...

"

Now, I mentioned in the last chapter the 10,000 sales made of a product I had licensed. At £49.95 a set – less my costs – 10,000 sales is a lot of money.

But they took time to get. Each time I sold some, I ploughed some of the profits back into more advertising, to increase the sales even more. At this rate though, this way of making money was never going to make me a millionaire – or a multi-millionaire – **quickly**.

If you're going to copy my business idea, you'll want to pay close attention as the next few pages will be the difference between you starting a mediocre business that earns you a living, or having a business model with the potential to make you an awful lot of money.

Let me give you a quick analogy, which perfectly illustrates how the method I'm about to share with you works. It's really very simple and it will help you to picture clearly what I'm about to run through with you in this chapter.

Remember back when you were a young kid? You hear a tune on the radio that you really like – from a new band that's just started up and is just getting their first airplay. In fact it's the first time you've ever heard this band, but you decide to buy their new single.

You like the single and you keep playing it. As a result, from that one single record, you became a bit of a fan of these new guys and you start wanting more of their music.

Then they release an album and you decide to buy that too. In fact, over the coming years you end up buying **EVERY SINGLE** that they produce and **EVERY ALBUM** too.

You also buy posters to go on your wall, you buy all of the **MERCHANDISE** put out by the record company – the mugs, the T-shirts, the smartphone cover. You may even consider joining the fan club. In short, you have become what marketers describe as **'in heat'** for everything associated with this band. You've become a member of this particular **'hungry crowd'** of fans.

From a marketer's point of view (the ones who make all the money) you're going down a very predictable path ... or to be more precise ... a **FUNNEL!**

You can see from the diagram that as a new fan you enter the marketing funnel through the wide end and, over time, travel through the funnel as you purchase more expensive, related products and merchandise for the band.

You can see from the funnel diagram how you can go from being a new fan, right at the top (that is, buying your first **single**), to spending a little more on a new **album** maybe a few days later.

Over time, as you get more and more interested in the band's music and, after buying more singles and more albums, you might then go on to buy a **Limited Edition CD Box** set of some of their earlier work. Or maybe you'll buy a **DVD** recording of one of their **live concerts**. In fact you might go to one of their **live concerts** too.

The point is, as you travel further and further down the marketing funnel, do you see how the products you're buying become more expensive?

You've gone from maybe buying a low-cost **£3** single as a new fan, all the way through to maybe a **£100** live concert ticket. Plus of course you've spent a lot of money in between on further singles, albums, DVDs, memberships, etc. So, in reality, that initial £3 has probably grown to a few hundred pounds ... and what's more, you are likely to be a fan for life, all the time the band keep putting out more good stuff.

When I set up my little business in my spare room at home, that's the model I used. I don't mean I am a musician selling my music. But every time I release a new product to a new hungry crowd of people that I have identified, I create a **marketing funnel** – rather than just selling a one-off, low-cost product.

That's how I made so much money so fast – by '**funnelling**'.

The funnelling formula

In my business, I'll start to attract new customers by offering them a low-cost product for, say, **£47**.

This little low-cost product is called a **front-end product** and might, for example, be in the form of a DVD set – maybe three DVDs – or maybe a printed manual and a CD.

But here's one way that my business differs from the music industry. Unlike the record company example, in my business when I sell a person that first low-cost product, I now have the **name and address** of that new customer. That name and address now goes onto my customer database on my PC. It is now very easy for me to contact that new buyer when I'm ready, by email or via the post, to offer them another related product (often at a higher price level); what is called a **back-end** product. It's just like the band analogy – the single is the front-end product and the album is the back end.

That one very simple formula, which I've used every day since starting my business, was the difference between me just earning a living and becoming a multimillionaire in a few short years.

I call it **FUNNELLING** because, as I intimated before, these basic steps mirror that of a funnel shape.

All your customers enter at the wide end of this funnel when they buy a low-cost product (*for example a £47 DVD*).

As they move through the funnel towards the narrow end, a *proportion* of those who bought the low-cost product will then buy the next **HIGHER-PRICED back-end product**. (In other words, not every music lover will go on to buy the album after they've bought the single.)

Of course, fewer and fewer individuals move down the funnel as it narrows (in the music business example, not all album buyers will buy tickets to live concerts) ... but then again those who do are buying more expensive products all the time.

So if, for example, my front-end product was a set of three DVDs on **How To Lose Weight**, which sell for £49 a set, and my little automated website sold 2000 sets:

That would bring me in £98,000!

From here my first back-end product might be a higher-priced DVD box set consisting of 20 DVDs. A **Personal Trainer in a Box** type of product to sell for maybe £297. Among the 20 DVDs in the set, I might have titles like:

How to Get Firmer Abs

How To Get A Flatter Stomach

How To Strengthen Your Core Muscles With Pilates

How To Build Muscle

and so on ...

Now, the costs of running off 20 DVDs with cases, printing, etc., would probably be no more than about **£35** for production and delivery of the package to the customer. So, in this 20-DVD boxed set example, it would give a staggering **PROFIT OF £262 PER SALE!**

Now, originally in this example, we had 2000 people buying the £49 DVD set. However, from this we might only get maybe around 10% of them buying the follow-up product (in this example, the 20-DVD boxed set). Which, in this case, might translate into web-based sales of 200 sets (10% of 2000 front-end buyers) at £297.

That would bring in another £59,400!

Following on from that, maybe your next higher-priced back-end product could be a **£1,997** *Lifestyle and Health Weekend Retreat* or a *Get In Shape Bootcamp*. These, of course, are just a form of workshop – a live event – the third product type I mentioned.

By the way, just like DVDs, you don't have to put workshops together yourself. Far from it. You are basically just using your website to promote someone else's workshop for which you'd get paid a percentage per ticket. This is called **joint venturing** (which I'll cover in Chapter 8) and the share of the profits is often a straight 50–50. So, for example, if you are promoting a £1500 workshop, your share would be around £750 per ticket.

Sell 50 of them through your back-end website and **YOU'VE MADE YOURSELF A QUICK £37,500** for a workshop you DON'T attend, DON'T put together, DON'T do anything for in fact. Do that every few weeks and you can see how the money can grow.

I've made over £ half a million in a single weekend promoting someone else's live event!

But let's get back to our **£1997** Lifestyle and Health Weekend Retreat example. OK, let's say you have a total of 70 individuals from the original 2000 who now go on to the retreat. In this example:

That would bring you in another £139,790!

So in total you have:

- £98,000 from the front-end product

- £59,400 from the first back-end product

- £139,790 from the second back-end product

Giving a final total of £297,190

As you see in this example, by using the funnel model (i.e. offering higher-priced products related to our original front-end product) our profits grow considerably for very little extra effort on your part.

If all we did was sell one low-cost product and then look for another hungry market and sell another low-cost product to them, and we kept doing this **we'd be missing out on huge profits.**

In our example, for instance, if we only sold the front-end *How To Lose Weight DVD* set at £49 our final total here would stay at £98,000 which means **we would have lost out on nearly £200,000** by not offering higher-priced back-end products to the same customers.

No, DON'T WORRY if all this sounds a little complicated. It's far, far easier than you might think. What I love about this business is that we DON'T have to create the products – we license them from someone else. We DON'T have to run off copies – a DVD duplication company can do that for us. We DON'T have to pack the boxes – a fulfilment house can do that for us. We DON'T have to download the orders, open the post, deal with customer enquiries, ship the products out to customers, process the payments, bank the cheques; that can *all* be done for us by a fulfilment house, in return for a modest handling fee per order!

The bottom line is that it is just a system that works. A system I've been using for over 15 years and which has made me millions of pounds and continues to make money even as I am sat here writing – while my business works in the background almost on autopilot.

For instance, last week (at the time of writing) one of my simple websites sold 142 sets of DVDs. These are a set of discs that sells for £199 a time, to people who have recently bought a low-cost front-end product. The DVDs for this **£199** product cost me around **£10** to run off copies and post to the customer. **So I'm making around £189 per set.**

So, on last week's sales alone – 142 sets at £189 each – I banked a **PROFIT of around £26,838 for the week** … and on just **ONE back-end product** alone!

Also, last week, another of my websites sold some higher-priced back-end products at £1697. In fact I sold 19 of them last week. Now these cost me around £50 per set to duplicate and have delivered to the customer, so I have a **profit of around £1647 a set**.

So last week I made a **PROFIT** of around **£31,293** on that one, high-ticket-price box of DVDs, plus the **£26,838 PROFIT** on the £199 sales too.

Giving me a TOTAL PROFIT of £58,131 for the WEEK! That's the power of funnelling.

> The bottom line is that it is just a system that works. A system I've been using for over 15 years and which has made me millions of pounds and continues to make money even as I am sat here writing – while my business works in the background almost on autopilot.

If you copy my business model, once you have created one funnel – with ever more high-ticket series of products appealing to one particular niche 'hungry crowd' – you can then build yet another funnel ... and then another.

For instance, you might have one funnel offering DVDs on *Weight Loss and Fitness,* another on *Golf,* with DVDs showing how to improve a person's golf, another on *How To Play The Drums* from beginners' DVDs through to advanced techniques, another on *Digital Photography*, another funnel offering DVDs teaching people how to trade online in *Stocks and Shares* and so on.

It's virtually limitless and there are literally TENS OF THOUSANDS of product niches out there that you could access.

The funnel in action

Take, for example, the financial crisis from a couple of years back. People were getting jittery and dumping their shares and looking for an alternative place to invest their money.

I had been marketing a low-cost introductory financial trading course (a couple of DVDs and a workbook) and had built up a good list of names and addresses of people who had started trading the stock markets. But with stocks and shares now going through an uncertain period, many of these people were looking for alternatives. In particular I found they were asking for information on how to make money in the *commodities* markets, on gold, coffee, soya beans, orange juice, etc.

So here was a hungry crowd of people all keen to learn quickly about investing in commodities. Armed with my new hungry crowd, I next looked around for a product to sell them. I quickly found a trader who could pull in several commodities experts to speak at a live seminar (again, workshops and seminars are one of the three ways that I deliver information to the 'hungry crowds').

We booked a function room in London and staged a two-day *Commodities Trading* seminar. Over 350 people attended at around £2000 a head (that's around £700,000 from ticket sales alone).

Now, of course, I didn't have to get up on stage and speak. I am not a commodities trading expert – I am just the person who knows how to put information in front of a hungry crowd.

We also hired a small camera crew to record the entire event. For those who couldn't make the date, we offered them an unedited DVD recording of the entire event instead – at the same £2000 price!

The attendees were so pleased with the quality of the information they received at the seminar that the main speaker got a standing ovation at the end for bringing together such great experts to speak. Many said it was the best financial training seminar they had ever attended.

Here's my point: the customers are delighted with the value they received at £2000 for a two-day seminar on a very hot topic at the time. We had loads of written testimonials from people praising the event. We were equally delighted with our £700,000 takings for the weekend. Both customers and promoters were happy. I guess that's been one of the reasons for my success over the past 15 years – I have always tried to over-deliver on my offers and make sure that the customer is always happy with the information they have purchased in whatever format – printed, digital or live event.

For the seminar, we also put together a simple manual for the attendees and DVD buyers, with charts, graphs and notes. And, finally, we provided a CD-ROM with some commodities trading tools and resources, which they could use to make their trading smoother.

So, from one hungry market of people interested in alternatives to trading in shares, came *three* types of information products: **paper** (attendee manuals); **DVD** recordings of the event plus digital products on **CD-ROMs**; and **workshops** (the event itself).

Oh, and after taking out all of the costs, we had a quick £643,000 in profit for a few weeks' work. And the reality is that I didn't have a lot of work to do for my share. I simply found experts able to provide *information,* offered that information to the list of hungry people (who originally entered my funnel through buying a low-cost product in the same financial trading niche), then I stood in the middle and banked the cash. Simple.

If I'd not had the funnel started – if I had tried to sell a £2000 seminar to strangers – there is no way they would have paid me. (That would be like making a marriage proposal on a first date!) But, as they already had a business relationship with me, when I offered them a hot new product (the seminar) they knew that it was being offered by someone who had delivered on his promises before, rather than someone they had never heard of.

That's how a funnel works. The first low-cost product **not only** delivers good value information to the new customer, but it also helps to start building a trusting relationship.

If something works, try it again!

Flushed with success from our foray into the niche market of commodities trading, I decided to add further training workshop products to the financial trading funnel.

I asked the trader if he could find other speakers. Within a few weeks, he had found another speaker who had a contrarian approach to trading, a real character from the US who people in that market would just love to see live on stage. We asked him if he would like to visit the UK to speak at an event in London. He agreed, in return for a fee and his air fare.

We then wrote to all the people at the top of the financial trading funnel again – *the identical hungry crowd* – offering a totally different event that would feature this new financial trading speaker talking about his rather different approach to making money on the markets – and we filled another seminar at £2000 a ticket. In the same way as before, we produced software and DVDs of the event – and a quick £395,650 profit.

Whilst this trading funnel was functioning – bringing in serious profits – I also had other funnels running that appealed to completely different niche markets: including one for hypnotherapy students and another for the dating market.

So you'll see how diverse this type of business can be. Please realise that I knew *nothing* about commodities trading, the stock market, hypnotherapy, or any of the other niche markets I have successfully tried – and I still don't.

But … I knew how to market DVDs, live workshops, etc. to hungry markets, using the system I had gradually developed as my business grew – and it's that system that you can copy to make a fortune from this too.

Probably, like me, before you picked up this book and gained an insight into this type of business, you'd not have had a clue that such a relatively simple business model existed or how it worked. When I was starting out I knew nothing about this business, or its processes.

I just had a gut feeling that someone, somewhere out there, knew a better way to live and a better way to make money than the career I had at the time.

I followed that gut instinct. I immersed myself in learning everything I could about the subject – learning from those who have already achieved wealth through *information publishing*, just as you are starting to learn from this book.

That's a winning habit by the way – being willing to invest time and money in your education. If I'd not invested time and money to attend that first seminar years ago, I would never have known about this type of business. That seminar was like a kick-start for me – a real wake-up call. That's what I have tried to do with this book too. To provide you with a good overview of the system I use as a sort of kick-start for you too.

Now I know I've been throwing down some pretty big numbers here – but don't let that put you off.

Always keep in mind that I started probably in the same position as you. I had no customers, no products, no business – and I had no idea what I was doing. **I simply copied a successful business idea – tweaked it and applied it in my own way.**

You see, no matter whether we are talking about large numbers or small, the business model is still the same

That's the beauty of it. It takes me almost the same amount of time

>
>
> **Always keep in mind that I started probably in the same position as you. I had no customers, no products, no business – and I had no idea what I was doing. I simply copied a successful business idea – tweaked it and applied it in my own way.**

to put a project together to sell one DVD set, for example, as it does to sell 10,000 sets.

You do the work ONCE. After that it's just a question of getting the offer out in front of more people. If you have a pay-per-click ad that is pulling a certain % conversion – and you want to increase your business – you just increase the number of times your ad is seen. If you are using direct mail and a particular letter is pulling a great response, you simply ask your mailing house to print off and send out some more letters to more people. Simple.

If I get one DVD order, I run off a copy for the customer. If I ramp up the numbers – and get 1000 orders – I ask a DVD duplication company to run me off 1000 copies (at around as little as 50p a disc!) Remember I'm selling 3 DVDs for, say £67. You can work out the numbers!

So, copy what I did: start off small, possibly doing everything yourself from home to keep your costs down; then, as the numbers grow, farm out some of the work to outsiders such as DVD duplicators, fulfilment houses, mailing houses, etc.

Now, of course, when you're starting out small you'll also want to know some low-cost ways to attract those new customers who will enter your funnel …

7

Low-cost Ways to Get New Customers

Billions of pounds are spent in the UK alone each year by advertising agencies on behalf of their clients.

But how many times have you watched an ad on TV and, just a few seconds later, can't remember what the product was that the ad was promoting?

Similarly, as I mentioned earlier, consider the glossy ads in magazines. We've all seen them. Two pages containing a huge panoramic scene with a small car in the bottom right-hand corner.

Maybe a copywriter has been paid to put three words on the page too, like *'Timeless Driving Elegance'* or whatever 'creative luvvy' nonsense – with a logo for the brand. Three words that the creative types at the ad agency think will help them get an award.

No website address, no QI code, no phone number, just the picture, the words and the logo.

No offer of a test drive, and no copy to tell you the benefits of this particular car over others. Nothing – just something you can frame and put on the boardroom wall at the ad agency, amongst the other self-congratulatory industry awards.

Ad agencies call this type of ad … 'brand awareness building'. They will persuade their clients, who have deep pockets, that they need 'brand awareness building' ads – to create awareness of the brand in consumers' minds so that when Mr Jones thinks it's time for a new car, he immediately thinks of their brand and pops into the branded car dealership to make a purchase.

In my business – despite the money I've made – I am not interested in wasting a single penny on a 'brand awareness building' ad. If I spend a single penny on an ad, I want sales … and I want them now.

Right from the start, when I placed my first tiny ad in a newspaper on my shoestring budget, the only reason I placed that ad was to get some instant sales. I needed the profits, to allow me to reinvest in another ad the following week – and so on.

> **In my business – despite the money I've made – I am not interested in wasting a single penny on a 'brand awareness building' ad. If I spend a single penny on an ad, I want sales … and I want them now.**

So, no award-winning 'brand awareness building' nonsense for me. No ad agencies. No copywriter writing three supposedly 'clever' words to go with a panoramic picture creatively shot on location somewhere halfway around the world. No framed masterpiece ads to go on my wall.

There's an old saying from a US department store owner, John Wanamaker in the 1800s, which says *'Half the money I spend on advertising is wasted; the trouble is I don't know which half.'*

I have a feeling that if ever those big glossy expensive ads had to include a way for the ad reader to respond and buy the product – as my ads do – most ad agencies would go out of business fast, as clients would very quickly suss that all that money spent was not actually bringing them a profitable return.

In my business I know **EXACTLY** which ads are pulling in my sales and which are not. Every time I have a new ad, I test it in a small way to see where and how each ad pulls. When I have an ad that works, I then switch all of my expenditure to the ads that ARE working and don't spend any on those that aren't (sounds so obvious doesn't it? – yet the 'big boys' have no way of knowing which of their ads are working).

The type of simple, low-cost, targeted advertising I use and that you'll want to use is called …

Direct response marketing

Let me explain. Let's assume we've found a hungry market, found a product to sell to that market and set up a funnel. What we need is to put people in the top of that funnel <u>fast</u>. People who will spend maybe £47 or £67 – or even £97 – on a front-end product, so that we can kick-start the process of creating a profit.

Back when I first started, the way I did this was to run a simple little classified ad in the newspaper offering free information about something that would solve the readers' problems, if they called a phone number and left their name and address. I would then have to send them a letter in the post explaining the offer.

These days of course the Internet has changed all of this for you and me – but the principles are still exactly the same. We no longer have to send anything in the post. Instead we can run a small, low-cost ad – either in the papers or online using pay-per-click advertising. This simple low-cost ad takes people to a specific website offering **one specific front-end product.** Not a catalogue site offering loads of options on what to buy. **Just a simple one-page site, <u>selling one front-end product</u>.**

Testing the market

I remember the day my Dad called me into his hardware shop and proudly showed me a display of a revolutionary new double glazing system. Seems a salesman for the company had talked Dad into buying a display stand full of stock of this new patented system. If I recall correctly, it was a sort of clear-plastic roller blind that could be pulled down over the window to form a second 'pane'. I'm not quite sure how it was supposed to keep out the cold – but it all looked impressive on the display stand that now took pride of place in the shop. I guess it was a low-cost version of secondary double glazing.

My poor Dad had probably committed a sizeable sum of money to stock the line. Bearing in mind that he needed to stock different-sized blinds for all the possible permutations of window sizes, this was some investment!

And, of course, the stock and the display stand had to be paid for within 30 days or so.

Dad bought the stock without first checking to see if anyone might want such a contraption – he liked the look of it and went on gut instinct.

Weeks, then months … then *years* passed and *no one* bought into the 'revolutionary' new double glazing concept. It seems they either weren't interested or they preferred traditional systems.

My father's testing of the market for this product (by stocking it for customers to see) had cost him dearly. He was now the proud owner of a load of stock that no one would buy! He eventually dumped the lot, unsold, when he closed his business.

Contrast this with the *Cash on Demand* business model I use. When I get a new product to sell, I normally know who will buy it, because (as I've tried to hammer home so far) I seek out hungry crowds of people (niche markets) ***before*** I decide what to sell them. And the beauty of selling information products is that we don't have to carry much stock before we know if anyone is going to buy them.

So, having identified who our customers are, we then target them with a cheap little classified advert, or some pay-per-click ads, pointing to a simple one-page website.

If the potential customers don't buy, you are out of pocket by the cost of the advert, which isn't a lot compared to my Dad buying a display stand full of stock for the shop.

Rolling out

What happens if you get some orders? Again, this is where the system pays hugely. With most traditional businesses you have to invest heavily in stock (usually in bulk to get the discounts that allow you to make a decent profit) and all before you've sold a single item.

Not so with a *Cash on Demand* type of business.

In the early days, when I did everything myself, if a customer made an order – a CD for instance – I would run off a copy on my PC, pop it in a sleeve and post it to them. If I got ten orders in a day, I simply ran off ten copies. I never had to buy a thousand discs at a time from a manufacturer.

Once I have an ad that works well in pulling people to a website – and a website that converts those visitors to sales – I am then ready to roll out the marketing using all of the techniques I teach my students in my monthly *Cash On Demand* course.

The point is, you have tested the customer's willingness to buy – you have tested whether the product will sell – **before** you commit anything more than a few pounds in test adverts. If it fails, you're not out of business or nursing your wounds while sitting on a load of dead stock. But if it sells you are then free to suck in as much money as possible.

Testing using *Cash on Demand* marketing methods makes all of this possible and makes this an ideal business to be in. If one product idea doesn't work, you've lost very little and can quickly move on to test the next idea.

Now, of course, once you have an ad that is pulling people to your website, it's important that your website is up to the job of grabbing the visitor's attention and holding that attention to the point where they will click the 'buy now' button and order.

There's nothing technically clever about this. You just need to make sure you have a few essential things in place on your site.

By the way, as I touched on earlier, most website designers don't know this stuff. They have come up from a techie background – learning how to code websites; or they come from a graphic design background – creating beautiful graphics. Neither route gives them any insight into what works from a marketing point of view.

Most website designers, given a free rein, will put together a large catalogue-style website for you: a catalogue site that starts off with a home page talking about your company and how wonderful it is – and tabs to each of your products.

That's not what works in the type of business you'll be copying here – yet so many website designers make a living selling such sites to ill-informed people.

Here are just a few pointers for the things I incorporate into my successful sites

Make it grab the attention!

A website designer will typically design a home page for your site that has a huge logo at the top and a large photo, with a little bit of text to describe the business and tabs to various pages. It is then up to the visitor to browse around the site to find what they want.

Forget it. That's for the 'brand awareness building' guys.

My front-end product website has one aim to achieve – and one only – to get a sale of my front-end product. No browsing, and no looking at other offers I may also have available. It's a site to give the visitor two choices – **buy or don't buy**. It's not a resource centre offering free information on a topic.

Now it's reckoned that we only have around three seconds to grab someone's attention before they click and go to another

> **The ONLY thing a person visiting your website is interested in is *WIIFM: What's In It For Me?***

site. So we go straight for the attention. No company logo – no pretty picture. No lines of tabs and a search box. No banners from other companies.

Instead – right at the top of the website – I feature a strong, attention-grabbing headline. There may well be a small picture off to the left to back up what is said in the headline – but the headline is the prominent thing that visitors first see when they log on.

Nothing is as critical as the headline and your opening paragraphs in your 'letter' on the website. The sole object of the headline is to get the customer to read what follows. It's a hook to keep them reading. If the headline doesn't grab their attention, the customer will never read the rest of what's written and won't even get to the 'buy now' button.

The ONLY thing a person visiting your website is interested in is WIIFM: What's In It For Me? So tell them what's in it for them – not how wonderful you think your business or products are.

I was once asked to help a housebuilder sell some houses. They had brochures that they sent out in the post to people who enquired. In this brochure they talked about the history of the company, when it was founded, the quality of their new homes, the after sales service they gave. But they were having huge problems selling their 1, 2 and 3 bedroom homes to first-time buyers.

I applied the **What's In It For Me?** principle.

We made up some large white signs – about a metre high – which we stuck on posts by the side of the main roads near the building site. They had just four attention-grabbing words on them, plus an arrow pointing to the housing site.

Move In For £50

That was all the sign said. It was a big, bold, attention-grabbing headline designed to catch the attention of passing traffic in a matter of seconds as people drove by.

That attention-grabbing headline told the passer-by one thing – what was in it for them. They could buy a house with just £50 down – no deposit, no legal fees, no stamp duty. For just £50 deposit they could buy a house!

We sold 21 houses that weekend – all from grabbing people's attention from those advertising boards on posts.

Your website visitor is like the guy in the car, whizzing down the road with loads to do that day. If you don't grab their attention as they pass by – you've lost them forever.

Know your hungry crowd and what they <u>want</u>

The key word here is 'want' not 'need'. In my experience, people prefer to buy what they **WANT**, not what they **NEED**.

Take your dentist, for example. Most people WANT two things from a dentist:

1. A nice bright white smile

2. Instant relief from pain if toothache strikes

Now what people NEED is a six-monthly check-up to look for early signs of problems that could lead to pain. But give someone a choice of visiting the dentist or doing something more fun – they'll probably choose the latter

So, in selling dentistry, I would sell the bright white smile first. I would sell what people WANT – not what people NEED. Once someone has bought your first product (the tooth-whitening session), you can then offer back-end products (the regular check-ups, the hygienist visits, the payment plans, and all manner of other dental offers).

Cars are another example. All we really NEED is a basic, unexciting but reliable vehicle to get us from point A to point B. But that's not what most of us buy or aspire to!

In fact if we were selling cars we might sell freedom and image and sex appeal!

When you know – *really* know – why people would want to buy your product, you can dip below the surface and start pushing the right buttons. (No point selling the benefits of an eco-car to someone wanting a gas-guzzling Bentley, for example. With one, you'd talk about the environmental issues, the huge mileage per litre of fuel used, etc. With the other you would talk about speed, handling, hand cut leather and wood veneer dashboards and exclusivity.)

Both are forms of transport – which is what people NEED. The difference is what they WANT.

So, in my projects, I always work on offering what people WANT – not what they NEED.

Use testimonials if you have them

We're a cynical lot these days. People expect you to be very overexcited about your own products and services. But your claims are just that – they're your claims and people may not believe them.

So, wherever I can, I incorporate testimonials from other people (on my website at **www.Andrew-Reynolds.com**, for example, I have over 3000 positive testimonials from students of mine). Each one, of course, has to be real – never make up testimonials. In my case, I hold on file a signed, written copy of each of those 3000 testimonials as proof.

Also, I always obtain permission to use the full names of anyone providing a testimonial. Using only initials ('J. D.') doesn't instil confidence in website visitors.

Now, when I was starting out, I had no testimonials for the products I was selling. I made a few sales without them. But as soon as I made sales, I asked those customers for their feedback and incorporated their written testimonials into my websites. When I hold my charity **Entrepreneurs Bootcamp** events – I always have two camera crews roving around during the breaks asking any volunteers to provide a 'live' testimonial on camera (if they are not too shy). Again, you can see some of these on the **www.Andrew-Reynolds.com** website.

You can do the same – asking people to record a simple video on their webcam at home and let you use it on your site. Or use written versions instead. I use both.

Offer a strong money-back guarantee

At this stage we are talking to brand new prospective customers – people who have never heard of us – never done business with us – people who don't know whether our products are going to be any good or not.

They see buying from us as a possible risk. We need to remove that risk.

I **ALWAYS** offer a money-back guarantee on a front-end product. Not some 'jump through hoops and prove to me you've done it' type of guarantee – no small print, no catch. I want to remove all of the risk for the purchaser.

I try to make my guarantees simple and straight forward:

> *'Study the XYZ DVD set at home and if you are not absolutely delighted <u>for whatever reason</u> – simply pop the set back to me within 30 days and I'll refund every penny of your £67 in full – no questions asked'*

And if someone sends it back in 32 days' time instead of 30? I still refund them. I am trying to build a lifetime relationship with that new customer. If they didn't like my product – no problem – they get their refund.

In one extreme case I once had a guy who bought a printed manual from me. It was a 200-page book printed on A4 paper delivered in a four-ring binder, which sold for around £97.

He sent it back within 30 days asking for a refund.

Now I <u>KNOW</u> that he photocopied the manual. How? Because he mistakenly sent me back the photocopied version!

What did I do? I refunded him (more for his cheek than anything else). The guy must have been most surprised.

So I didn't make any money on that front-end product.

Now I could have simply crossed his name off my database of customers – or worse, got into a fight with him about the copying. But I didn't. I had the **'back end'** in mind …

I always included him in any future back-end offers I made to my new front-end customers. To my delight, that same guy has gone on to spend over £30,000 with me over the years, on back-end offers. That's £30,000 I wouldn't have had, if I had not refunded him or I'd called him names and deleted his details from my computer.

So, offer a strong money-back guarantee to remove all risk from the potential new customer so you can start building a lifetime relationship with them. I am amazed when marketers don't do this. I make far more sales through offering a guarantee. Look at these typical figures:

- Without guarantee: Sell 100. No refunds. Net sales 100.

- With guarantee: Sell 160. 20% refunds. Net sales 128.

So not only have I ended up with 28 more net sales through offering the guarantee, making my immediate profits higher, but I also have an additional 60 brand new customers to offer other products to in the future

It's a no-brainer.

These are all techniques I have used successfully to secure new customers who are then likely to go on and purchase back-end products from me using the funnel model.

These new customers get entered onto my customer database.

Building a customer database...

You might recall that I mentioned I first came across this type of business when I was invited to a seminar in the US and met a quietly spoken gentlemen who showed me how to make $30,000 a month working from my spare room.

But at that same seminar I also met another successful home-based entrepreneur, from Australia ... a guy who was already running the type of business that I wanted to start myself.

We spoke for a while but the one thing that stands out in my mind is one phrase, one key point he made to me:

'You need to build a customer database, mate!'

Now I had no idea what he was talking about ... but, at the risk of looking like the village idiot, I asked him to explain. I'd just learned about **funnel marketing**, now here's a guy from Australia telling me I need a database too. Eh?

Well I needn't have worried, as it all turned out to be so simple. All he was saying is that when customers start buying the products my website is offering, I need some way of automatically storing their contact details – not just their email address but their postal address too.

I found out that it can be something as simple as using a **Microsoft Excel Spreadsheet**.

In fact, when I started – because I was setting up my new business on a shoestring – I kept it even simpler by recording my customers's names and addresses on cards in a plastic filing box. Not very high tech I know, but it did the job.

So why keep a customer database?

Because your database of names and addresses is **your livelihood for the future**.

Follow the funnel model. A new customer buys our front-end product. Their name goes onto our customer list/database. In a week or so we then take all the names of people who bought last week and send them our first back-end offer (could be via an email or by post).

Then a few weeks later you do the same with your next back-end offer.

But, of course, if you never kept a customer database to begin with, all you'd end up with would be a few low-price front-end sales. You'd never make the really big money.

Don't worry about this too much. A **database** sounds like it could be complicated, but as I said it is basically just a list of names and addresses (and email addresses) of people who have bought from you – which also gives you a means of tracking what they have bought and when – so you can offer them related products rather than the same ones again.

Remember, when I started my little business **I HAD NO CUSTOMERS – ABSOLUTELY NONE!** But over the years I gradually built up my own customer list … my own buyers' *database*.

And many of the customers who bought products from me 15 years ago when I first started … because I treat them well and have always over-delivered on my promises to them … still buy from me today.

Which is why, at the end of the day, the most valuable part of your business is your database of customers. In effect you are building a business asset that can reap rewards for many years to come (something we call 'the lifetime value of the customer').

> **Remember, when I started my little business I HAD NO CUSTOMERS – ABSOLUTELY NONE!**

Now it's taken me time to build my loyal customer database – it didn't happen overnight …

But as always there is a shortcut to get you up and running faster …

8

The **Fast** Track

“

I wanted to speed up the whole money-making
process without paying out a load of money…

”

When I first started my business in my spare room at home, back then I launched a simple front-end product … it was a simple video tape showing people **How To Make Money On eBay** (which was a new phenomenon back then), plus two free bonus tapes showing how to make money online in other ways (now, of course, these would be DVDs rather than video tapes). They featured an American guy sharing how he made money at home.

Using the techniques I've touched on in previous chapters, I gradually built a small database of targeted customers … a list which today incidentally stands at over 50,000 customers (thanks to something that I'll show you in the next chapter).

But remember I had started out exactly where you are now. I had no customers … no database … no track record.

Yet, within about a year of offering my little front-end product, I had around 3000 customers who had bought this low-cost front-end product.

But, thinking back to the funnel model, I knew that the big profits are not generally in front-end products. The massive profits come from the follow-on products … the back-end products.

However, at the time – since I was just starting out – all I had ready to offer was this one cheap little video set product. No back-end product to speak of.

But I wanted to speed up the whole money-making process without paying out money for a licence to a more expensive product I could use as a back-end.

The next level

So here's what I did even though I didn't have my own licensed back-end product.

Actually it was this position I found myself in that really introduced me to a whole new side of the business – the business of **Joint Venturing**.

This is what happened.

As I'd been putting my product out, a few people *in the trade* had seen my material … seen my adverts … read my *write-ups* in the press …

As a result they emailed me and asked if I'd be interested in offering one of their own products to my new customers.

Now, I'll be honest: I didn't know what I was doing at the time. No one had ever taught me what I'm sharing with you now (*I had to make it up on the spot and learn as I went along*). Which is why the first guy I did a joint venture with must have been laughing all the way to the bank.

He offered to pay me **10% on all the sales he made** as a result of **ME** sending his offer to **MY** customers. Of course, I naively agreed. I thought this would be a good deal … *money for old rope* as it were. All I had to do was send his offer out to my new customers – and he would send me a cheque for 10% of everything my customers bought from him.

So I sent out his brochure to my list – and people bought. We sold a lot of his products.

But the reality quickly hit me that he made a huge amount of money and was doing nothing at all, while I was doing all the work, giving him some of my customers and only making a paltry *10%* for all my efforts.

DOH! (Told you I was no genius.) When I emailed him asking him about this, he explained that he'd taken years to develop his product – and how 10% is better than what I had before, when I was selling NOTHING to my newly acquired customers.

I could see his point: it was better to make something rather than nothing and I am grateful that he introduced me to the world of joint venturing. But still I had a gut feeling that this wasn't the best way of running joint ventures.

So I decided to do the reverse …

And, instead of someone coming to me with their products eager to sell them to my list, I decided to do it the other way around and actively look for other individuals or businesses that might have suitable back-end products.

Products that would suit the 3000 front-end niche-market customers I had.

I did this by looking on the Internet, and scanning through adverts in magazines and newspapers that were selling products/services that were related in some way to my product niche.

That's when I first discovered that there are huge numbers of products and services you can joint venture, not just with my line of products, but with almost any you'd care to mention.

So, when I found them, I simply emailed a handful of the companies to begin with.

In my monthly *Cash On Demand* course, I show my students some email samples that they can adapt and copy to get their own joint ventures.

WWW.CASH-ON-DEMAND-COURSE.COM

This single email that I sent to these companies produced a great response. For example, one guy who emailed me back ran a little **website design company** that provided dealerships allowing people to sell *web design services* to small businesses.

This was the start of discovering how to make a huge amount of money quickly through joint venturing ...

The cost of the website dealership product they were offering was around **£3000**. I thought this would be a great, natural, back-end product for my video set, which was about how to use the Internet to make a living.

In other words, I had 3000 people here who wanted to start their own Internet-based business and, with the website company, I'd found a ready-made business with whom they could do just that.

Furthermore, the mark-up on the dealership that the website company was offering was pretty high. Naturally, they had a few costs. For instance, they had a very good training package for their new dealers, which included binders of information, video training, CD-ROMs, etc.

In addition, the company provided a free bespoke website for the new dealer.

Yet all this only carried a cost to the website company of around £200

In other words, there was a potential **PROFIT OF £2800 PER SALE.**

So here I was presented with a great opportunity to test the water with a great potential back-end product and I could move away from the ridiculous 10% joint venture I'd been on with the earlier individual's product.

No way was I going to help them (for a paltry 10%) to make a profit of around **£2800** from my new customers – the new customers I had worked hard to get – and a profit that they would not otherwise have had. So I emailed them and boldly asked them for **50% OF THE PROFITS**.

I quantified this in my email by adding that, if just **10%** of **MY** front-end customers bought their product (i.e. 300), on a 50% profit share basis, this would mean **they'd be sitting on a quick £420,000+ PROFIT** for doing **NOTHING** except fulfilling the new orders I produced for them.

Obviously I'd also make £420,000+ WITHOUT having to put together my own back-end product.

All I had to do was send a short email, or one-page letter, to my **3000 customers** recommending the website dealership. The web company would provide all the sales materials and handle any sales queries and customer questions, etc.

Well the quick estimated **£420,000+ profit** for the guy running the website company obviously struck a note and he agreed straight away.

I must admit that this was the first time I had been actively involved in seeking out a joint venture, which is why once I had his email confirmation I was feeling really chuffed.

I must admit, though, that when I switched off my computer – when I thought about what I was doing – I turned to jelly. Have you ever seen those movies where the guy does some huge deal, looks all confident, then rushes to the men's room and throws up? Well that's exactly how I felt.

Why? Well remember, I had no experience of this ...

I started to think: here I am, a humble 'little guy' who's only just started his business and sold a set of low-cost little videos, a guy running the whole thing on a part-time basis from a tiny desk and an old PC, in his spare room at home.

Yet I had just demanded 50% of the profits from any sales made to my customers – and they'd happily agreed!

Of course, all my joint ventures are like this now and it's become the norm. For example, let's suppose you had a product that carried a **£99 PROFIT** and I put it out to **40,000** of my customers with a strong recommendation letter bearing my name.

With a **10% conversion** that would produce **4000** sales – or **£396,000** – something that would probably take **less than three weeks** to achieve.

On a 50/50 basis, **I'd get to keep £198,000 and YOU'D GET A CHEQUE FOR £198,000**.

I'll talk about how you and I can do joint ventures together once you have your new business up and running. But, before that, I'd like to take a moment to give you some advice about the lure of money.

Reputation is everything

Please DON'T BE DRIVEN PURELY BY MONEY.

DON'T promote anything just for the sake of it (because, for example, you think you can make a quick **£ half million**) **IF** that product is **NOT** something you can honestly endorse or would use yourself.

I've seen so many people, even major multimillionaires, make huge mistakes through endorsing some poor product or service to their list of customers just for the money. This **NEVER** works in the long term, no matter how tempting it may be.

For example, I knew a famous newsletter publisher who had a **VERY** loyal subscriber list. His customers hung on every word he said. They couldn't wait for his next issue.

Then, one day, he promoted one of those silly multi-level marketing 'pills and potions' offers to his list. No doubt he'd been driven by the lure of residual income from thousands of his customers who he anticipated would become his MLM 'down-line'.

The result?

His customers deserted him in droves. Overnight his integrity had gone. Each month he'd been writing to them as a friend yet, in a flash, in one moment of stupidity, he'd alienated them.

He literally went from banking HUNDREDS OF THOUSANDS OF POUNDS A MONTH to less than a thousand ...

In an instant he virtually closed his business because of that stupid, greedy error of judgement.

That's the danger of endorsing something to your database of customers just for the money. **DON'T EVER DO IT!** There's no need to, anyway, especially when you can make millions of pounds doing this properly with quality information products.

For example, imagine when I first started out, if I'd blindly written to my brand new customer list endorsing the website company **WITHOUT** first **TESTING** their training materials, and checking out some of the websites they had made in the past.

Imagine if I'd just been dazzled by the possibility of making myself an easy **£420,000** for sending their marketing materials to my small list of new customers.

Well, the result would have been that – yes, maybe – I would have made a quick £400,000 or so, but I would have lost all my customers and credibility.

For the sake of £400,000 I would have lost out on £50,000,000 (£50 million).

The reputation for integrity that you build over the years counts for so much. If you go for the quick buck – by endorsing poor products or questionable schemes/companies – then you will have a short business life.

So when you are approached by a person asking if you would like to do a joint venture with them, or you decide to approach someone to do a joint venture with you, make sure you do a few simple checks first.

Send off for their product; actually buy a retail version from them as a mystery buyer. See if they deliver on their promises.

> **That's the danger of endorsing something to your database of customers just for the money. DON'T EVER DO IT! There's no need to, anyway, especially when you can make millions of pounds doing this properly with quality information products.**

Try the product. Does it actually work? Does it do what is claimed?
Do they honour their guarantees? Send it back for a refund if there is a money-back guarantee. Did they pay up? How did they treat you?

If you have any doubts at all about the company or the product, don't do the joint venture. It's your name on the line – your reputation – and that counts for so much in business.

I once had a series of tech support hassles with a piece of software I was using in my business – a shopping cart program to run my online sales. I was getting nowhere with the tech support helpdesk people, so I tracked down an email address for the CEO of the company and got in touch. He phoned me.

I started to explain the hassle I was having and that my business was suffering because his software wasn't working properly.

He said he'd not called about that, as his tech guys were 'on it'. Instead, he wanted to talk to me about offering his software to my customers for a % of the profits.

I was stunned. Here's a guy whose software is not working properly, and he's asking me if I would like to ignore that and make some money by offering this same flaky piece of software, which doesn't work properly, to my loyal customers.

I was outraged. I explained to him the meaning of the word **integrity** – and I changed my shopping cart software supplier that same day.

Yes, I could have made some money, but my customers would no doubt have had the same tech issues and would have then questioned my own integrity. If I recommend something to my customers it is because it works well and is something I am happy to have my name associated with.

Taking it to the next level, even faster

So, as you've seen, I learned very quickly the power of joint venturing, and how I could offer other people's products to my growing list of customers, for a decent % of the profits.

But, back then, my biggest problem was the time it was taking to build my list of customers in the first place.

An ad in the paper might bring me a few hundred new customers a month. However, at that rate I'd be old and grey before I ever achieved a large enough database of customers to make me my fortune. As each ad ran, of course, I reinvested the profits into more promotions and was gradually building the business. But it was by no means a fast process. If I'd had a spare £ million or two, I could have used that to roll out my promotions, which would have helped to speed up the process.

It was like a real-world chicken-and-egg situation – I needed more customers to make me money, but I needed money before I could get the customers.

Then I discovered the way to get loads of customers without needing to find a penny for marketing.

> **Then I discovered the way to get loads of customers without needing to find a penny for marketing.**

I found companies with large databases of customers in my target niche.

Now, these companies often run on a slightly different business model. These 'traditional' publishing companies survive by selling truckloads of low-cost products to new customers. One month they will run a promotion for a book on *Stock Market Trading* then, the following month, they'll be running a promotion for a book on *How To Pick Hot Tips At The Races*.

Their business model is: lots of sales to lots of people for a small amount of money per sale. No funnel, just thousands of low-cost product sales.

It's a living. One of these companies that I have done a lot of business with over the years has a huge packing and mailing house. Picture large, high tables and loads of ladies wearing tabards, all looking like my favourite old dinner lady from school, stuffing envelopes with promotions for that month's particular hot, low-cost product.

With the staff to pay, the overheads of the warehouse and packing centre, plus their offices and other overheads, these guys need to run one project after another.

Now they do well but, as you've seen, it's quite different to my model: I don't have to worry about what promotion we can sell thousands of, next month, at £45 or whatever. My funnel model means that we only have to do a few projects a year to make more money.

So, these companies have large databases of customers all of whom have bought low-cost products (what we would consider to be front-end products). And what these companies are always on the lookout for are yet more low-cost products to sell to their huge lists of customers, just to keep the 'factory' going.

When I was still building my business, I approached one of these companies.

By the way, remember when I was starting out I had nothing – no track record, no million-pound business ... nothing. But I was determined to do business with one of these companies.

When I first met them, I hid my old banger of a car around the corner so they wouldn't know that I was just an ordinary bloke who had recently started in his spare room and didn't have much money. I wore a suit and tie and played the part of the successful business guy. Imagine if I'd gone in there dressed casually, parked my rust-bucket car outside their head office reception and told them I knew nothing but could they offer one of my products ... and I'd let them have half the profits. They'd have shown me the door!

So, as an aside, if you copy my ideas for yourself and want to develop relationships in this business, even if you are just starting out: be yourself, but be sure to put your best foot forward! As with the website you use to show your customers your product or the package you send them – make sure you also look the part when you meet joint-venture partners for the first time.

Anyway, back to the story. I arranged a meeting with this company and I took along a copy of a promotion I had been running for a low-cost product of mine. It was a subscription product – in other words, customers paid a monthly subscription and received the product month by month.

The profit each month was around £20 per subscription.

Now the beauty of a subscription product is that you only have to sell it ONCE and people's subscription payments then come in automatically … month after month, after month. So money turns up every month without you having to do anything in terms of advertising or marketing. You simply send the subscriber the latest month's package when the next payment turns up.

So, if a subscriber stays with you for maybe three years, on a product that makes you a profit of around £20 per month, you have a potential profit of £720 per subscriber.

Now, before I sought out a joint venture with these larger companies, I needed to test-market the product (after all, they are not going to risk their money on something that's not been proven; on something that we don't even know yet if the customers will buy).

So I tested the market with ads, with direct mail, with some online marketing … and the numbers looked good.

Armed with those numbers, I met the company owners and talked to them about a possible joint venture, of plugging my product into their monthly promotional system, and sharing the profits.

They agreed to test it.

In fact, whereas my own tests would be, for example, a small ad or perhaps a tiny mail shot to maybe 500 people, these guys said they would test it …

… with 50,000 (fifty thousand!) of their best customers.

Of course the HUGE benefit of someone joint venturing to *their* list of customers is that they have a relationship with their loyal customers. On a joint-venture promotion, therefore, if there is a covering letter or email with the promotion, endorsing and recommending this new product, it adds greater weight to the offer as it is being recommended to customers by someone they trust. It's a bit like a friend suggesting you take a look at the product.

And they do. On that 50,000 test, we had a much higher response than I ever would have got if I had contacted those customers myself without that company's endorsement.

In fact the response was about three times what I had been getting with my own promotions. So, if I'm giving away half of the profits to the joint-venture partner, but I'm getting three times as many sales as I normally would, I'm actually in a better position financially.

It's a real no-brainer.

And, of course, the REAL beauty of this deal is that these new customers, who have bought my product through this joint venture, now go into the top of *my* own marketing funnel.

I have, say, 3000 new customers from the joint venture, who have now just bought my front-end product … and you know now the money involved when I then take those new customers and sell them a back-end product (which could, for example, be the venture with the website company).

In fact, in some cases, I have been happy to give away more than 50% of the profit on those front-end products – just to get the new customers. Think about it: if I am handed 3000 new customers for my product on a plate, and it hasn't cost me a penny to get those customers, I could actually afford to give away 100% of those front-end profits, just to get those new customers on board and into my funnel system.

Because, once I have those 3000 people who have bought from me, I can almost immediately offer them a back-end product or two and make a huge profit that way. I've already shown you earlier how I pulled in some £480,000 from just 3000 new customers. So if I did the same again – for customers that cost me nothing to acquire – I'd have banked a quick £480,000 (nearly half a million pounds) … all from joint ventures.

In my monthly *Cash On Demand* course, I show you how to do other forms of joint venture – including one where you have no products of your own and no customers either (**www.cash-on-demand-course.com**).

But we're getting ahead of ourselves. For now, let's move on as there's something else that led to my success in this business… something you need too, if you are to copy what I do fully …

If You Want to **Get Rich** – Copy the Rich Bloke

I found someone who had already achieved what I wanted to do – and was prepared to show me how they did it, so I could copy them…

In this book I've shared some insights into my system for making money so that you can copy them.

There's one other element that I consider crucial to my success, though: having a good coach and mentor to learn from – having someone who's already done it themselves – showing me how to do it too.

For example, when I decided a couple of years ago that I really should learn to swim, a decision brought to a head when I bought a large house with a swimming pool, I tried to brave the pool by myself but ended up going nowhere. I'd cling to the safety of the pool side, afraid to go out of my depth. But then I found a swimming coach who was prepared to help me – to teach me how to get rid of my fear of water and to do some basic strokes. Here was an expert swimmer and someone who was prepared to spend time in the pool with me to help me learn.

A couple of times, I must admit, I nearly gave up. I recall one particularly memorable session: we were in the pool and he asked me to spread out my arms and legs in a star shape, lying on top of the water. He then asked me to exhale – quickly blowing out every last drop of oxygen in my lungs that I could possibly find. I sank downwards to the bottom of the pool. Then he did something you'd only want a coach to do – someone who knows what he's doing! He stood on me – pinning me to the bottom of the pool, even though I'd exhaled all the air in my lungs. For what seemed like several minutes I lay there on the tiled surface at the bottom of the pool – unable to move with his foot resting on my back. Then, just as I started to tense up and panic, he let go and I made it back to the surface.

The lesson he so dramatically wanted to show me was that, even when I thought I had not a single drop of air left in my body, I could still survive for a few minutes underwater as the body has sources of oxygen other than what I think I have in my lungs. It was a very dramatic demonstration. Something I never would have let anyone but a professional swimmer and coach do for me. In fact, if he'd told me what he was going to do before he did it, I might not even have allowed him to do it – out of sheer terror. But it worked and it's a lesson I have remembered to this day. I am so grateful to my swimming coach for that.

I no longer have a fear of water. I no longer stay in the shallow end. I no longer gingerly work my way round the sides hanging on for dear life. And I am no longer embarrassed when friends come round for BBQs at the pool. In fact, because I found a coach and did what he told me, I can now swim lengths of the pool completely underwater – something that feels so absolutely natural for me to do – and which four or five years ago I would have said was totally impossible.

It's the same in business. If someone had told me, back in my corporate days, that instead of just getting by financially each month I would soon be making over £1 million a year – yet only working a few hours a week – I'd have said they were nuts. I had a burning desire to do it – but I had no idea *how* to do it.

Just like my swimming coach, I needed someone who could take me by the hand and show me step by step how to do each little part. I needed someone who could show me what they did and then help keep me on track while I tried to copy their methods for myself.

I remember a teacher at school teaching me this principle with a simple story:

Imagine you're with a group of soldiers in the midst of a battle somewhere.

You and these soldiers are being pursued by an enemy who is slaughtering everyone and everything in their path.

If you don't escape, it's certain death …

Now, your only chance of survival is to cross a hidden minefield. If you can just get across you'll not only survive, but a wonderful life of freedom awaits you on the other side.

Arriving at the edge of this minefield the sergeant orders the first six of the troops to cross.

Unfortunately, five of them don't make it and perish. But, thankfully, one gets across safely. Only one guy gets to freedom on the other side. The sergeant now turns to you … it's your turn to go.

Do you say, 'I'm going to make my own path thanks'? Or would you perhaps follow the paths of the five soldiers who had just perished in front of your eyes?

OF COURSE NOT!

So what do you do?

You follow EXACTLY in the footsteps of the soldier who made it …

I'm sure you would very precisely and carefully put one foot after the other, in the footsteps left in the soil by the guy who got through the minefield safely to the other side.

So why should you act in any other way if you want to better yourself?

Do you follow the guy living in mediocrity? Do you follow the guy who's running an unsuccessful business?

Do you follow the guy who's operating a franchise but who's running around like a headless chicken just to make a wage?

Do you follow the guy who's making £20,000 a year running a shop working six or seven days a week, 12 hours a day?

Do you follow your mates at work – the individuals who you are currently working with, in a full-time job? Do any of them have your ideal lifestyle? Are any of them truly happy?

Do you follow your friends, family and acquaintances?

Are any of these leading a life of financial freedom? Leading the life you seek?

Do you follow the small business advisor at your bank who lives on an average housing estate, drives an average car, and makes an average income?

Do you follow an accountant who's got even more bills and debts than you?

Or do you follow the individual who has already become a multimillionaire and who leads a life of GENUINE FREEDOM?

Looking at it that way, the answer becomes obvious.

And it is. It's what you need to do. It's what I did myself. I found a guy who had made it … who had achieved what I wanted to achieve. He allowed me to copy what he did and I just followed in his footsteps. It's what all the successful individuals I know have also done. They find someone who has succeeded and follow in their footsteps.

It's what my own successful students have done – they copied the business model that I taught them, either in my live training workshops or via my monthly step-by-step courses – and applied it to their new businesses.

Several of my successful students pulled in over £1 million. In fact several pulled in far more.

- A former alarm salesman, who I taught, copied my system and with my guidance pulled in over £10 million.

- A part-time musician who I taught, who studied my system and started up in his spare room at home after facing redundancy at work, pulled in over £7 million.

- A former DJ who I agreed to mentor, copied my system EXACTLY and banked over £3 million working from his desk at home.

- A former call-centre worker, who I taught, copied my system and, with my help in the background, banked over £1 million from her kitchen table at home.

And all because they understood that to succeed you need to follow in the footsteps of someone who has already done what you want to do. They each took the time to copy my system for themselves.

Of course, they didn't need to work full time on this. When I started my business, for example, I'd handed my notice in at work, but I still had to work out that notice period. So I simply got my business set up in any spare hours I had at weekends, or in the evenings after work. I just ignored the TV for a few months and focused on copying the business system I had been shown.

You could do the same.

I hope that, as you've been reading these pages, I've given you a great insight into the business I now run – and that it's given you a kick-start and possibly changed your thinking about how money can be made by ordinary down-to-earth people like you and me.

And if it has, I'd be delighted to share more with you and to guide you as you get started, just as I have for the people I've just mentioned. I'd be happy to act as your coach and mentor – to make sure you go in the right direction. Because it is so easy to put this book down now and to go off in the wrong direction – if you don't have someone to keep you on track.

It's a bit like my fitness trainer. If he didn't come round regularly to put me through my paces, I'd not bother. I'd drift along and get nowhere with my fitness. But because I have someone who has achieved what I want to achieve – in this case a level of personal fitness – who is prepared to call round to my gym at home a couple of times a week, to keep me on track – I get to achieve what I want in life. And when he's not there I am spurred on to do my exercises, knowing that he'll be back tomorrow to see how I have got on.

That's what I would like to do for you, if you are serious about copying what I do. In a book of this size there is no way I can teach you every single thing I do. As I mentioned earlier, this book is intended as a kick-start – to show you an alternative way of doing things – an alternative way of making money that's not based on some daft theory, but on actual proven results.

I would be happy to teach you my complete system in more detail and to help you along the way to keep you on the right track – just as I did for the £ million students of mine that I have mentioned in this chapter. None of them had any previous experience in this business. Yet, through copying my system and having me teach and coach them month by month, they went on to each bank well over £1 million.

To get us started I'd like to send you three DVDs and some other written materials, with my compliments. I don't want any money for these, by the way. If you'll just pick up the tab for the postage, I'll be happy to send

> " ... this book is intended as a kick-start – to show you an alternative way of doing things – an alternative way of making money that's not based on some daft theory, but on actual proven results. "

you these materials straight away absolutely free. Just go to **www.free-package.com** and let me know where to send them and I'll get them to you so we can get you started.

Now, I want you to think very, very seriously about what I've just said here ... because it's not only the kind of opportunity that seldom, if ever, comes along. After all, if I am not the person you choose to teach you how to run a business, who else will you turn to for advice and help?

Unfortunately, most people bumble along in life, taking advice and guidance from all sorts of people – many of whom don't know what they are talking about.

In fact, my own Dad was no different in his business life. There were many reasons why his business failed, but one important one was the people he surrounded himself with.

He NEVER had a mentor to learn from. Someone who had succeeded in the type of business my Dad wanted to run. Someone who was living the kind of lifestyle my Dad would have loved to lead. Instead he looked to his bank manager and his accountant for input and advice on how to run his business.

Now, let's look at that for a moment. Let's look at those two individuals. Are they really qualified to advise on business?

On the surface, it appears, an accountant must be. After all, accounts are at the heart of a business. A bank manager must be too, surely, as he deals with the banking side of many, many businesses of all sizes across a broad spectrum of business niches.

Ideal people to give you advice on how to run and grow your business?

OR PERHAPS NOT!

I recently had coffee with a guy who I went to college with when I was 18. We chatted about what he had been doing since leaving college.

Turns out that, straight after college, he went to work for a bank. And, 36 years later, he is STILL working for a bank. His entire working life – and therefore his ENTIRE business-life experience – straight from school and college – has been working for a bank.

And guess what side of banking he's involved in? Would you believe, working with small businesses?

So, if I was a small business, banking with that bank, looking for more advice on how to run my business, he would be my first port of call. He would be the person I could look to for that advice as he is 'in banking dealing with small businesses'.

But something's wrong here, surely …

At the end of the day, the guy is just an EMPLOYEE who has NEVER run a business in his life.

Yet he is employed by a bank to advise businesses. That's how the banking world works – CRAZY – in fact, it's COMPLETELY NUTS!

Here's a person who knows absolutely NOTHING about running a business. His advice is based on theories they get taught at 'bankers training school' or wherever they teach their staff.

His advice is not based on doing it for himself. He gets paid a safe salary each month (and some banks pay their small business advisers a commission for selling you their products and services, like insurances, and giving other 'good' advice too).

Actually, he's one of the LAST people you should consider seeking advice from about how to run a business and make money.

And that's ditto for an accountant … as I mentioned briefly in Chapter 1.

Similarly, my Dad used to meet with his accountant regularly as well as his bank's business adviser.

Over a cup of tea they would discuss my Dad's business plans – and he would make the mistake of asking, 'So what do you think, John?'

John, the accountant, would then give his advice and, because he was a professional person who knew about business, my Dad would heed his advice.

I remember he would come home after one of these meetings – all fired up. 'John says we should do (XYZ or whatever) …'

But, hold on again. What the hell does John the accountant really know?

He's just a guy whose job it is to deal with numbers. He's basically like the guy at a cricket match who keeps score. He has NO EXPERIENCE of actually ever having played the game himself.

He's just watched from afar and dealt with the scores.

Bear in mind that, whether a business does well or does badly, accountants tend to get paid either way. It's the same with bankers. They get their money either way, and often up front too! So they lead a cushioned existence.

Up until recently I had such an accountant. We'd meet maybe once a month to look at how my business was doing financially. Then, over a coffee, he'd start to ask questions and give advice. None of which I took, thank goodness. I just listened out of politeness, to be honest.

Anyway, I just got on with making my millions while it turned out that this accountant's practice was in bad shape. In fact, at one point, he came to me to borrow some money to keep it going. He couldn't run his own business properly – yet he was positioning himself as someone to take business advice from.

And believe me, he's not the only accountant that's nearly gone belly up.

It should be obvious, anyway, not to listen to these types of people. After all, ask yourself, have you ever met a rich small business advisor or accountant?

NO, NEITHER HAVE I. Still, my poor old Dad, bless him, never ceased to listen to these professionals.

Another mistake he made, and which you should also guard against making, was to belong to a small business association.

Might sound impressive but, looking back, I realise that many of the members of that association my Dad belonged to were struggling small business people themselves. They were people just like my Dad who weren't making much money.

They would get together and have meetings and social events. They'd inevitably chat about business. So, when my Dad had an idea, he'd chat with his fellow members about it and get their feedback.

But, once again, hold on there Dad! These other association members are failing business people. He was getting input and advice about business from people who were failing at business themselves.

Today, thanks to the Internet, we have to be even more on our guard about who we listen to.

Actually, it's worse than ever and is something I became aware of when I ran several discussion forums online over the years. Each one, I'm glad to say, I eventually closed and I never visit a forum myself these days, either. My advice – avoid them like the plague.

Why? Because the negativity that permeates forums is ridiculous. When I used to take a look at them I could actually feel myself being pulled downwards by others – sucked into this dark cloud of negativity.

Originally, I naively thought it would be great to have a discussion forum, where people wanting to start a small business could chat and meet.

But the reality, which took me a long time to wake up to, was that the only people who posted on the forums were life's whiners and whingers. People who, no matter what, will always see a negative and try to bring everyone else down too: life's scoffers. I'm sure you know the type.

I suppose I shouldn't have been surprised, as people who are succeeding in life simply don't waste their time moaning and groaning and posting on forums.

And if the successful people aren't on the forums, to balance out the scoffers, the forum goes into a downward tailspin of negativity.

So turn a deaf ear to the moaners, whiners and whingers of life.

Don't waste your time listening to the bloke down the pub, who always has his own jaded opinion on everything – an expert at nothing but an opinion on everything – a person who spends all of his or her time propping up the bar and spreading negative nonsense to anyone who will take time to listen.

Remember that when I came back from the US, all fired up with enthusiasm for what I had just been shown, my Dad – with his business background – my work colleagues and my friends all scoffed at the idea of me setting up a business in my spare room.

But £50 million+ later I'm so glad I followed my gut instinct and ignored their advice. You'll want to ignore the scoffers and the negative people too.

In contrast, you should surround yourself with positive people and, if you can't do that, get yourself some audio CDs or DVDs of people who have succeeded in life. Immerse yourself in positivity. I do that, even now. If ever I need motivating to get a new project done, I simply immerse myself in listening to – or watching – successful people.

I'll turn off the TV and, instead, pop in a DVD recorded during a seminar. I'll watch someone who has been successful with a way of doing something, so I can not only learn what they do, but I can also get myself fired up again. If you are serious about copying my business model, you'll want to do the same. Hopefully this book has provided you with a good kick-start and has opened up some new ideas to you; ideas that you can copy to start a business of your own. Now you'll want to immerse yourself totally in learning everything you possibly can about this business. To help get you started, as I mentioned earlier, I'd like to send you three FREE DVDs and some other materials, with my compliments. Go to **www.free-package.com** and just let me know where you'd like me to send them.

On that website you'll also find a link to OVER 3000 POSITIVE TESTIMONIALS … from people who have attended some of my entrepreneurial events I have spoken at – and you'll also be able to watch some of the videos, which I'm sure you'll find inspiring.

Anyway, the point I am getting at is that you have to open your eyes and ears and be aware of who you are listening to in your life.

It's so important …

For example, when I wanted to start my business I didn't talk through my plans with an accountant or a bank manager. Instead I sought out an entrepreneur who had already done what I wanted to do, and I did everything I could to learn from him, so I could copy his business model myself.

That entrepreneur, as you now know, was the quietly spoken American gentleman I mentioned. He became my teacher and mentor, albeit at a distance. Since I obviously couldn't keep flying back and forth to the US every month, I figured that the best way to learn from this guy was to subscribe to a monthly newsletter he wrote. Each month I'd receive his newsletter through the post and each month it was like a little kick up the backside for me – pushing me in the right direction. From time to time he'd send me videos too. Watching these was like having him with me in my lounge, talking me through a particular topic – perhaps showing me how to use a new piece of software that could help my business grow.

In addition, on the rare occasions my mentor spoke at seminars or workshops in the US, I'd fly 3000+ miles to attend (paid for out of the profits my little business was already producing).

That's how dedicated I was to becoming wealthy. It's been my experience that if you want to succeed, you need to totally immerse yourself in your chosen passion.

I surrounded myself with anything he had written or recorded so that I could learn his methods, before he eventually retired.

If you have found this book interesting. If your gut is telling you – like my gut told me back then when I first met the guy who would become my mentor – that this is a business idea you could copy for yourself – I would be happy to help you build your own business.

Just go to www.private-consultation.com, let me know where to send it and I'll send you a certificate that entitles you to a FREE one-hour 'business builder' consultation with me. I don't want a single penny for this consultation. There's no catch. I'll send you this certificate and some other materials, including the three DVDs I mentioned earlier – and I don't want you to pay me a penny for them. If you'll just pay the postage, I'll be happy to send everything to you with my compliments, for you to keep.

Why would I offer to do that?

Think about the last chapter. I mentioned the joint ventures I have done with some of my students. They studied my system, copied what I do and set up their businesses. In the long run, many of them then did joint ventures with me, in which both of us made money.

So you'll see that it is in my interest to help train you and coach you as you get started – as I hope that we'll do some joint ventures together in the future. There's no obligation on either of us to do so, of course.

In this book I've laid out all of the main ideas I have used in my business – from a start-up in my spare room, to a multimillion pound business. You can use the ideas in this book as a kind of kick-start to your own business and work on your own. But there may be times when having a joint-venture partner and a mentor to work with might help you grow your business faster, just as it did when I was starting out. It certainly helped all of the £ million students I've mentioned in these pages. Remember, none of them had done anything like this before. All of them started out by copying my business methods – and I was happy to help each of them with joint venture deals too, once they were up and running.

Keep in mind what I mentioned at the beginning of this chapter – how I had a fear of water and how, if friends of mine had told me that a few years later I would be able to swim lengths of my pool underwater, I would not have believed them.

I got someone who was an amazingly good swimmer to teach me, and I copied what he showed me and was able to achieve things I never would have thought possible.

I just needed that help – that kick-start – to get me in the pool and to lower my head below the water line.

Starting a business seemed daunting when I first thought about doing it – but with the right teacher and coach it was much simpler than I ever could have dreamed of.

You just need to jump in …

Let's
Get Started
Today

*If you've not done it already – let me know
where to send your FREE package of DVDs
and other materials at
www.free-package.com*

When I was asked to write this book, my publisher asked me 'what is the biggest, most meaningful thing that making all of this money has done for you? What's the one thing above all that you can point to, as meaning the most to you?'

I started off this book talking about what money has allowed me to do – I mentioned buying my Mum a lovely house and giving her financial freedom after a life of scraping by and making do. That, to me, is the most important thing that my business has done so far.

For you it might be something completely different. You may have a totally different goal in life – or someone special that you would like to help. How many times have you said 'I'd love to … if only I had the money'?

Copy the ideas in this book and you might just be able to …

I've also mentioned my Dad a lot in these pages – showing you the business model that he used, compared to the one I use. I've tried to show what happens if you choose the wrong business model to copy. And, of course, I've tried to show you what happens when you choose the RIGHT business model too … how even an ordinary bloke like me, with my woodwork and drawing O-levels, can become a multimillionaire. It's something that would make my Dad very proud if he was still around to see it.

Maybe you're someone who would like to make your Dad proud – whether he's around or not.

Maybe you have some other goals in life that you want to achieve too. Not just to look after your family and close ones – but to reach out and help others too. Help that you can't give if you are desperately trying to make money just to keep your own head above water financially.

I always promised myself, when I was growing up, that if ever I made any serious money in life I would do something sensible with it – rather than just fritter it away. I've kept that promise.

This morning, in a township of tin shacks in South Africa, 400 or so children went to school with food in their bellies provided to them by a soup kitchen that I fund. They also took with them a sandwich for lunch and will get dinner tonight from the soup kitchen too. (You'll see them on the FREE DVDs I've mentioned that I'd like to send you.) Those children don't go hungry – because a very ordinary guy, living halfway across the planet, happened to stumble upon a great way to make money and a few years later was therefore able to help them financially.

Similarly, hundreds of sick children have been treated in a children's ward at Great Ormond Street Hospital – a multi-bed specialist treatment room that I raised all the money for, through my business. I wonder how my Dad would feel if he could see the plaque on the door of that room bearing his son's name. Certainly, it feels weird to be leaving such a legacy – a hospital room that will help so many for years to come. Starting my little business in my spare room a few years earlier brought that about too.

When I began this book with the chapter 'It's not just about the money!' – that's what I meant. This book is not just about showing you the type of business I run so you can copy what I do and make yourself a pile of money. It's about what you do with that money too.

It's about making the money by copying what I do, then doing something useful with that money, once you've secured your own financial position and helped your family and those close to you. It's about having a vision of what you would like to do with the money you make.

That's what I did – I paid off all of my debts first, got myself financially secure with my house and car all paid for, etc. Then I helped members of my family and a few friends too. After that, I went on to achieve my childhood promise of doing something useful with the money I managed to make. Running this business enabled me to achieve that goal.

Tell me, what's your goal? What are the things you want to achieve in life? What are you doing right now that will get you closer to achieving that goal? Are you any closer now than you were a year ago?

Time is ticking by.

You know, when I was little boy, my Dad took me to Heathrow airport to see Concorde take off. I remember him saying 'I wonder where they're off to' and, I remember so clearly, thinking 'Sod that – I don't want to know where they are going – I want to be on the damn plane!'

Just a few years ago – after I'd made my first £million from my little business – I fulfilled that ambition by flying to New York and back on one of the last flights of Concorde.

If I'd not taken immediate action 15 years ago, when I stumbled across this unique way of making money – if I'd not got off my backside and done it right then and there – that trip on Concorde would still be a pipedream. You see, time moves on – it's moving right now as you're reading this book.

If I'd left it a few years, I would have missed that particular opportunity to fly on Concorde as, of course, it's been taken out of service now.

> **When I began this book with the chapter 'It's not just about the money!' – that's what I meant. This book is not just about showing you the type of business I run so you can copy what I do and make yourself a pile of money. It's about what you do with that money too.**

My Dad, standing behind that counter in his little hardware shop, gazing out of the window daydreaming, always used to promise himself – 'when I retire, I'll …'. But he never got there. Time passed by while he took no action and just daydreamed.

The title of this book is *Copy This Idea*.

> **If you want to make a difference – not just in your own life, but in the lives of others around you – you need to make a start right now too.**

You need to copy what I did. I'm not talking about just starting up a business using the things I've shown you in this book – but copy the fact that I took action immediately, when I found what I was looking for, and got my business started.

I didn't fly home from the seminar in the US and put my book full of notes and the handouts from the workshop up on a shelf to gather dust – telling myself that 'one day I'll get around to that'… I didn't listen to the negative people telling me it would never work.

I knew it was what I wanted to do – so I took immediate action. I made a start.

If you want to make a difference – not just in your own life, but in the lives of others around you – you need to make a start right now too.

Don't put it off. There's nothing more important on the telly tonight. There's nothing on your Facebook page that won't wait. No Tweets that are more important than this.

In fact, right this minute, you could do what I did back then before I started. I wrote myself a wish list. Just a simple list of things I wanted in life. I listed them out – a house worth £half million, £500,000 in cash in the bank, a top-of-the-range BMW and a few other things. The main thing is that because I took action – every single thing on my wish list came good. Within five years of starting, I had moved into a large house that, in fact, I paid over £1 million for – in cash! No mortgage – no borrowings. I just paid cash. I had well over £500,000 in the bank too – and on the drive was my new BMW. It all came true ...

> **Don't put it off. There's nothing more important on the telly tonight. There's nothing on your Facebook page that won't wait. No Tweets that are more important than this.**

And it's all because I found a guy who had a great way of making money that gave me a kick-start and I took action to learn from him – to copy his ideas. That's what I have tried to provide you with here in the pages of this book, a great kick-start to move you onto a path that could lead your life, and the lives of those close to you, in a totally different direction

You know, I still have occasional nightmares when I'll wake in a cold sweat – panicking because I've had a dream that I was back working for a living in a full-time job and all of this new life had just been a dream.

Then I open my eyes and look out of my panoramic bedroom window at the sun rising over a calm sea with a horizon that stretches as far as I can see to the left and to the right – and I realise that, no, it wasn't a dream. I really did give up working 60+ hours a week in a full-time job I hated – I really did start a business in the spare room of my little three-bedroom house on the local estate – I really did trade in my old car that had 200,000 miles on the clock and now drive a Bentley that I bought new and paid for in cash – and I really am a multimillionaire now.

Copying this business has allowed me to do some extraordinary things in life. Most of all it's given me freedom.

Now it's your turn. Time for you to take action right now. Time for you to **copy this idea**.

I wish you all the success you deserve and hope to work with you in the future.

About the
Author

Andrew
Reynolds

Award Winning Start-Up Entrepreneur
Andrew Reynolds

Born and raised in a caravan, Andrew Reynolds attended school on the local council estate. He wasn't a strong performer at school, leaving with only 4 O-levels (including woodwork and drawing). After school he drifted from one meaning-less and unfulfilling job to another, including working as a clerk in the health service, a trainee estate agent, a shop assistant, a soft toy salesman, and various other attempts at employment, before starting a career as a trainee in the housebuilding industry.

A few years before he decided to start his own business, Andrew was virtually penniless and on the edge of despair.

Yet, despite all this, using the simple ideas he outlines in this book, and starting part-time in his spare room at home, Andrew quickly became a self-made millionaire at the age of 45 and a multimillionaire by the time he was 50.

He went on to win the coveted **Surrey Business Person of the Year Award** together with the **Small Business of the Year Award.**

Further awards have followed, including **Business Event of the Year** and **Best UK and International Conference** for his sold-out **Entrepreneurs Bootcamp** – a charity event which he held at the O2 Arena in London. Attended by 8000 aspiring home-based entrepreneurs from all over the world, this event raised over £700,000 for the Make-A-Wish Foundation children's charity.

He has since appeared on television a number of times, on Sky, BBC1 and BBC2. He became a Patron of the Prince's Trust and has been commended for his business initiatives for young people, such as **Make Your Mark with a Tenner** – an initiative he funded to teach young people about making money on a limited budget and about the importance of social responsibility.

Social responsibility is a subject Andrew is passionate about, which is why – more than just creating his own personal financial success – he has also used the ideas he shares in this book to raise millions of pounds for national children's charities such as Great Ormond Street and the Make-A-Wish Foundation along with other local charities including Disability Initiative and the Phyllis Tucker Hospice.

Andrew funds a soup kitchen in Cape Town, South Africa, which feeds around 400 young children three meals a day. He has also helped build more than 20 new brick homes to replace the temporary shelters made from old tin and scraps of wood in the surrounding shanty town of Khayelitsha.

And to think this all started when he stumbled upon a unique and highly profitable way of making money that he'd never even heard of at the time.

Today, having banked over £50 million, he invites you to **COPY HIS IDEA** for yourself; to kick-start the lifestyle you personally dream of by following in his footsteps; and to give you the freedom to do the things you feel most passionate about.